Creating
ENGAGED
Employees

It's Worth the Investment

William J. Rothwell, PhD, SPHR, CPLP Fellow
Catherine Baumgardner, PhD
Jennifer Myers
Woocheol Kim, PhD
Olga V. Buchko
Naseem Saeed Sherwani, PhD
Rashed A. Alzahmi

ASTD Press is an internationally renowned source of insightful
and practical information on workplace learning, training, and
professional development.

ASTD Press
1640 King Street
Alexandria, VA 22314

Ordering information: Books published by ASTD Press can
be purchased by visiting ASTD's website at store.astd.org
or by calling 800.628.2783 or 703.683.8100.

Library of Congress Control Number: 2014945565

ISBN-10: 1-56286-910-8
ISBN-13: 978-1-56286-910-6
e-ISBN: 978-1-60728-429-1

ASTD Press Editorial Staff:
Director: Glenn Saltzman
Manager, ASTD Press: Ashley McDonald
Community of Practice Manager, Human Capital: Ann Parker
Associate Editor: Melissa Jones
Editorial Assistant: Ashley Slade
Text and Cover Design: Lon Levy
Printed by United Graphics, Mattoon, IL, www.unitedgraphicsinc.com

Table of Contents

Acknowledgments

William J. Rothwell would like to thank his wife, Marcelina, and his daughter Candice, for being there for him. His son, Froilan Perucho, is not to be forgotten either, even if he is stuck in the cornfields of Illinois, for just being the wonderful person he is.

All the authors of this book would also like to express appreciation to Jong Gyu Park and Aileen Zabellero for their help in coordinating our work.

Preface

William J. Rothwell and Woocheol Kim

Employee engagement has become a cause célèbre. For some—such as managers who are not willing to devote any time or effort to it—it is indeed a controversial topic. But others see a worldwide economic crisis brewing, and employee engagement may be the answer to one of our generation's greatest workforce needs. After all, according to Gallup's well-known annual survey (Gallup Q12), many workers feel overworked and underappreciated. Improving employee engagement is one way to fight that trend.

Based on my work experience, many of us have had professional experiences with employee engagement. When I was in charge of human resource development (HRD) and employee relations (ER) at a global company, some of the employees were energetic, willingly put effort into what they did, and were deeply involved in their work. They demonstrated enthusiasm, inspiration, and pride in their jobs, despite work demands and pressure. All in all, they successfully achieved their goals on individual and team levels. There were other people, however, who were always torpid, unwilling to exert effort unless strongly urged to do so by managers, and were less involved—only doing the minimum amount required to avoid negative feedback and adverse consequences. These people often failed to achieve their goals and could not meet work deadlines.

Why the difference between these two groups? Although there are many reasons, employee engagement is one possibility. If we look at employee engagement, the former group might be regarded as engaged people or an engaged workforce, whereas the latter group might be regarded as disengaged people or a disengaged workforce.

With these distinctions in mind, this book uses practical wisdom and scholarly research to examine the following questions: What is employee engagement? Why are people engaged or disengaged? How can we measure employees' engagement? Can organizations help their employees be engaged? How can organizations help and maintain engaged employees without burnout?

Organization of This Book

The primary aim of this book is to examine the importance of employee engagement according to the scholarly and practical literature in human resource development (HRD) and human resource management (HRM).

This book opens with an Advance Organizer to help you zero in on which of the seven chapters has what you're looking for.

Chapter 1 reviews diverse definitions of employee engagement, describes types and core components of employee engagement, and explains the antecedents and consequences of employee engagement using a conceptual model. It also offers a brief research history on the topic and suggests possible future research opportunities.

Chapter 2 explains the importance of employee engagement, addressing three important questions: Why should we care about employee engagement? How do business leaders and academic researchers view employee engagement? And what are the possible outcomes of an engaged workforce?

Chapter 3 reviews well-known methods of determining an organization's level of employee engagement: the Utrecht Work Engagement Scale (UWES); the Shirom-Melamed Vigor Measure (SMVM); the Shirom-Melamed Burnout Measure (SMBM); and Gallup's Q12. This chapter also shares some insights for further research on work engagement concepts by reviewing past studies.

Chapter 4 offers an explanation for the relationship between work engagement and job performance, which has received much attention from business leaders and academic researchers. The chapter goes on to introduce the concept of workaholism, clarifying what it is and how it relates to employee engagement. It also explores the strategies in which employers stay focused on "what to do" and "how to do it" and engage their employees to improve their performance. Finally, the chapter offers techniques and strategies for engaging and re-engaging disengaged employees.

Chapter 5 focuses on ways to create an engaged work culture. It poses the simple but profound question, what does an engaged workforce look like? It then goes on to discuss ways to build engagement, and how to strike a balance between work and personal life.

Chapter 6 explains the barriers to employee engagement in association with organizational culture/climates, leadership styles, and performance. It offers guidance on how to overcome barriers to employee engagement by providing recommendations for leaders regarding organizational culture and climate, as well as supportive and transformational leadership styles.

Chapter 7 describes the future of employee engagement. This chapter discusses how to bridge the academic and business models of engagement, examines and challenges the job demands-resources (JD-R) model, explores whether employee engagement is a concept or a proven theory, and queries whether the control of employee engagement lies with the organization or the individual. The chapter closes with a recap and assumptions about the role of employee engagement in the coming years.

Advance Organizer

William J. Rothwell

The Organizer

Complete the Organizer before you read the book. Use it as a diagnostic tool to help you assess what you most want to know about employee engagement—and where you can quickly and easily find it in this book.

Directions

Read each item in the Organizer below and circle true (T), not applicable (N/A), or false (F) for each one. Spend about 10 minutes answering the questions. Be honest! Think of employee engagement as you would like it to be—not what some expert says it is. When you finish, score and interpret the results using the instructions at the end of the Organizer. Share your responses with others in your organization and use them as a starting point for conceptualizing employee engagement. To learn more about one of these topics, refer to the number in the right column to find the chapter in which the subject is discussed.

The Questions

	Do you believe employee engagement in this organization is already:	See chapter:
T N/A F	Based on a specific definition of employee engagement?	1
T N/A F	Linked to credible research on employee engagement?	1
T N/A F	Linked to strategically important issues to the organization?	2
T N/A F	Measured according to credible approaches?	3
T N/A F	Linked effectively to individual performance?	4
T N/A F	Linked effectively to organizational performance?	4
T N/A F	Linked effectively to organizational culture?	5
T N/A F	Implemented in a way that will address likely barriers to success?	6
T N/A F	Distinguished effectively from job satisfaction?	7
T N/A F	Considering future trends that will change the nature of work and workers?	7
___	Total	

Scoring and Interpreting the Organizer

Give yourself one point for each "T" and zero points for each "F" or "N/A." Total your score and interpret it as follows:

- **Above seven points**: Your organization may already have an effective employee engagement program. While improvements can be made, your organization has already matched many best-practice employee engagement principles.

- **Four to seven points**: Improvements could be made in your organization's employee engagement practices. On the whole, however, your organization is already on the right track.

- **Below four points**: Your organization is far away from effective employee engagement.

1
Introduction

Woocheol Kim

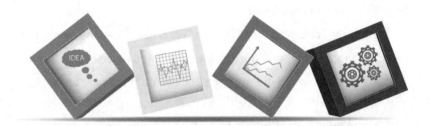

What Is Employee Engagement?

The term employee engagement has been receiving a great deal of attention from scholars and practitioners in many fields, including human resource management (HRM), human resource development (HRD), organization development (OD), psychology, and business (Kim, Kolb, and Kim, 2012). One reason for this attention is that organizations tend to expect their workforces to be proactive, show initiative and collaboration with others, take responsibility for their professional development, and commit to performance with high quality standards. Thus, employers need employees who are energetic, dedicated, and absorbed in their work—an engaged workforce (Bakker and Schaufeli, 2008). Furthermore, engaged employees are very attractive to organizations because of their higher productivity levels, profitability, safety, and low turnover rates and absenteeism (Shuck and Wollard, 2010). Despite the importance of engagement to organizations, however, scholars and practitioners can't agree on its definition (Schaufeli and Bakker, 2010).

Since the first formal definition of engagement was introduced by Kahn in 1990, many scholars and practitioners have focused on conceptualizing it. Engagement has been described in different ways and has been associated with such varied terms as employee engagement, work engagement, job engagement, role engagement, and active engagement, as shown in Figure 1-1.

Kim, Park, Song, and Yoon (2012, p. 3921) examined the diverse definitions of engagement in Figure 1-1 and revealed three major themes:

- The main scope of employee engagement focuses on work roles, activities, tasks, or behaviors.

- The definition attempts to capture individual employees' psychological states, such as commitment, satisfaction, enthusiasm, fulfillment, involvement, and motivation.

- Core components of the construct are related to organizational consequences (for example, performance).

They also synthesized the definitions of engagement into the following statement: "employee engagement is a cognitive, emotional, and behavioral state of an individual employee that crosses three dimensions: job engagement (i.e., with tasks and work), relational engagement (i.e., with people), and organizational engagement (i.e., with an organization) in pursuit of positive work outcomes" (Kim et al., 2012, p. 3924).

Figure 1-1

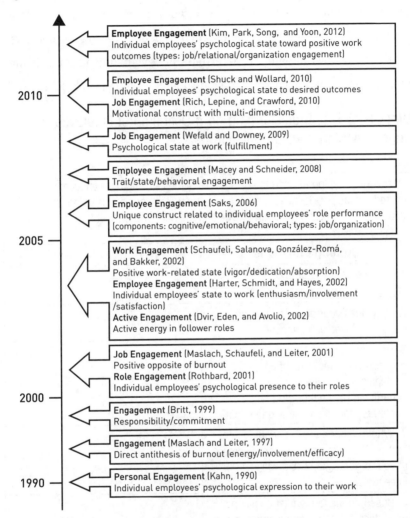

Employee Engagement (Kim, Park, Song, and Yoon, 2012)
Individual employees' psychological state toward positive work outcomes (types: job/relational/organization engagement)

Employee Engagement (Shuck and Wollard, 2010)
Individual employees' psychological state to desired outcomes
Job Engagement (Rich, Lepine, and Crawford, 2010)
Motivational construct with multi-dimensions

2010

Job Engagement (Wefald and Downey, 2009)
Psychological state at work (fulfillment)

Employee Engagement (Macey and Schneider, 2008)
Trait/state/behavioral engagement

Employee Engagement (Saks, 2006)
Unique construct related to individual employees' role performance (components: cognitive/emotional/behavioral; types: job/organization)

2005

Work Engagement (Schaufeli, Salanova, González-Romá, and Bakker, 2002)
Positive work-related state (vigor/dedication/absorption)
Employee Engagement (Harter, Schmidt, and Hayes, 2002)
Individual employees' state to work (enthusiasm/involvement /satisfaction)
Active Engagement (Dvir, Eden, and Avolio, 2002)
Active energy in follower roles

Job Engagement (Maslach, Schaufeli, and Leiter, 2001)
Positive opposite of burnout
Role Engagement (Rothbard, 2001)
Individual employees' psychological presence to their roles

2000

Engagement (Britt, 1999)
Responsibility/commitment

Engagement (Maslach and Leiter, 1997)
Direct antithesis of burnout (energy/involvement/efficacy)

Personal Engagement (Kahn, 1990)
Individual employees' psychological expression to their work

1990

Employee engagement and work engagement are the most popular of the terms shown in Figure 1-1 and are often used interchangeably by scholars and practitioners (Shuck and Wollard, 2010). Thus, this book does not distinguish between them. The term employee engagement is preferred by the human resources field.

Scholars have different perspectives on engagement and the employee engagement construct seems to be multi-dimensional. In that sense, how one defines employee engagement may depend on how it is perceived in a certain environment. To determine how your organization defines employee engagement, use the guiding questions found in Worksheet 1-1.

Worksheet 1-1: Brainstorming on a Definition of Employee Engagement in Your Organization

Directions: Keeping in mind the diverse definitions of employee engagement offered in Figure 1-1, think about the ways in which your organization or your HR department regards employee engagement and answer the guiding questions.

Guiding Questions	Write Your Answers
1. Who cares about employee engagement in your organization?	
2. Why does your organization care about employee engagement?	
3. How do you care about employee engagement? What kind of policies, strategies, or activities do you currently implement or plan to implement for employee engagement?	
4. What might be the important factors that contribute to employee engagement in your organization? (List at least three factors.)	
5. Based on the four earlier questions, what does employee engagement mean to your organization?	

Types of Employee Engagement

Most definitions and studies regarding employee engagement conceptualize it as a singular concept, but other perspectives see it as a multiple concept. For Saks (2006) employee engagement is comprised of job engagement and organizational engagement. Macey and Schneider (2008) described it in terms of trait, state, and behavioral aspects.

Kim et al. (2012) divided employee engagement into three core dimensions: job engagement, relational engagement, and organizational engagement. They explained that job engagement is a task-oriented dimension focusing on the engagement between individual employees and their tasks and work; relational engagement has people-oriented dimensions focusing on engagement among people's relationships; and organizational engagement is an organization-oriented dimension focusing on engagement between individual employees and their organization.

When it comes to the timeframe perspectives of employee engagement, Sonnentag, Dormann, and Demerouti (2010) explained work engagement as occurring during a specific moment or short-time period, and trait work engagement (that is, general work engagement) as a state that occurs over a longer timeframe. While many research studies focus on general work engagement, others have targeted specific timeframes for employee engagement, such as daily employee engagement and weekly employee engagement (Bakker and Xanthopoulou, 2009; Bakker and Bal, 2010).

Core Components of Employee Engagement

Employee engagement can take many forms. In the literature, most definitions of employee engagement are described in association with affective (or emotional), behavioral (or physical), and cognitive components

(Kahn, 1990; Kim et al., 2012; Macey and Schneider, 2008; Rich, Lepine, and Crawford, 2010; Saks, 2006; Shuck and Wollard, 2010). In addition, Schaufeli, Salanova, González-Romá, and Bakker (2002) further characterized employee engagement as vigor (high levels of energy and mental resilience), dedication (sense of significance and enthusiasm), and absorption (fully concentrated and deeply engrossed).

The Evolution of Employee Engagement

Understanding the concept of engagement and examining its relationships with other research variables in which organizations are interested has been evolving since 1990. Looking at where empirical studies have been and where they need to move forward would be more beneficial for us to effectively apply the concept and its influences to the workplace.

Empirical Research

Even though the term engagement was coined and introduced by Kahn in 1990, it received very little attention from researchers until early 2000 (Shuck and Wollard, 2010). Since then, much effort has been put into understanding and studying the subject. In an integrative literature review Shuck (2011) found four primary approaches: need-satisfying (Kahn, 1990), burnout-antithesis (Maslach, Schaufeli, and Leiter, 2001), satisfaction-engagement (Harter, Schmidt, and Hayes, 2002), and multidimensional (Saks, 2006).

In another empirical literature review, Kim, Kolb et al. (2012) focused on the relationship between work engagement and performance. After examining 20 empirical studies, they found that 11 had reported either a direct or indirect relationship between engagement and performance, seven examined work engagement as a mediator, and two examined the relationship mediated by another variable.

Furthermore, Kim et al. (2012) investigated 31 empirical studies on employee engagement and reported that almost half (14 studies) investigated employee engagement as a mediator, 12 looked at employee engagement as either an antecedent or a consequence, and five investigated employee engagement as both an antecedent and a consequence. They also found that employee engagement could be anticipated in advance and enhanced through the efforts of individual employees and their organizations by providing job resources and personal resources, and they concluded that employees' improved engagement would have a positive relationship with organizational outcomes, such as job performance (in-role and extra-role) and lower turnover intention.

Future Research

Despite the importance and popularity of employee engagement in organizations, there have not been many empirical studies on the topic (Saks, 2006; Shuck and Wollard, 2010). In the future, more effort should be made to clearly and comprehensively explain the subject, so as to help organizations facilitate and maintain their employees' engagement by providing and supporting appropriate resources. Scholars believe that these activities will lead to more positive organizational outcomes. Although instruments have been developed to measure employee engagement, including the Utrecht Work Engagement Scale (UWES) (Schaufeli et al., 2002), some have reliability and validity issues and others have issues with measuring preconditions of employee engagement (Jeung, 2011). Therefore, more attention should be paid to developing and measuring employee engagement in a robust manner.

Antecedents and Impacts of Employee Engagement

The antecedents of employee engagement could be any variables or constructs that might have an influence on employee engagement either directly or indirectly. Bakker and Demerouti (2008) described job resources and personal resources as antecedents of employee engagement through the job demands-resources (JD-R) model of work engagement. They maintained that sufficient job resources (for example, autonomy, feedback, and coaching) and appropriate personal resources (such as, optimism and self-efficacy) could help to enhance work engagement. Recently, Wollard and Shuck (2011) further attempted to comprehensively identify antecedents of employee engagement by reviewing extant literature and classifying the antecedents into two types—individual and organizational. They reported 42 antecedents: 21 were individual-level antecedents (such as, value congruence, motivation, and self-esteem) and 21 were organizational-level antecedents (for example, leadership, organizational rewards, and organizational culture).

Because these antecedents could be regarded as key predictors of individual employee engagement, an organization's HR department may want to consider them when establishing any engagement-related HR policies or developing activities to enhance employee engagement.

Researchers have revealed the positive impact employee engagement has on various organizational outcomes. For instance, employee engagement influences:

- organizational or individual performance (Bakker and Bal, 2010; Bakker and Demerouti, 2009; Halbesleben and Wheeler, 2008; Harter et al., 2002; Medlin and Green, 2009; Rich et al., 2010)

- self-efficacy (Luthans and Peterson, 2002; Richardsen, Burke, and Martinussen, 2006)

- turnover intention (Jones and Harter, 2005; Koyuncu, Burke, and Fiksenbaum, 2006; Saks, 2006; Schaufeli and Bakker, 2004; Wefald et al., 2011)

- psychological or mental health (Koyuncu et al., 2006; Laschinger and Finegan, 2005)

- job satisfaction (Koyuncu et al., 2006; Saks, 2006; Wefald et al., 2011)

- absenteeism (Schaufeli, Bakker, and Rhenen, 2009)

- employee creativity (Zhang and Bartol, 2010)

- proactive behavior (Salanova and Schaufeli, 2008; Sonnentag, 2003)

- organizational commitment (Hakanen, Bakker, and Schaufeli, 2006; Llorens, Bakker, Schaufeli, and Salanova, 2006)

- organizational citizenship behavior (Rich et al., 2010; Saks, 2006).

Conceptual Model of Employee Engagement

Bakker and Demerouti (2008) suggested a notable conceptual model of employee engagement known as the JD-R model, which consists of work engagement, its antecedents, and impacts.

However, we suggest using an integrated conceptual model of employee engagement, which is based on the antecedents and impacts of employee engagement (Bakker and Demerouti, 2008; Wollard and Shuck, 2011). The suggested conceptual model framework (Figure 1-2) is comprised of employee engagement as a mediator, between its antecedents (the independent variables) and its impacts (the dependent variables). In this model employee engagement is comprised of three dimensions—job engagement, relational engagement, and organizational engagement—which are based on the definition from Kim et al. (2012). In addition, the antecedents consist of individual antecedents and organizational antecedents (Wollard and Shuck, 2011), and are related to job and personal resources as well as job demands. Impacts include diverse constructs (for example, in- or extra-role performance, turnover intention, employee creativity, and psychological/mental health) based on the extant empirical research, as described in the previous section.

Figure 1-2: Conceptual Model of Employee Engagement

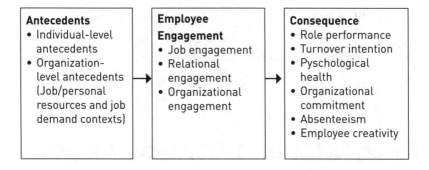

Antecedent variables in the conceptual model framework are the factors that may predict and either positively or negatively influence the engagement of individual employees in an organization, as well as explain a wide-range of outcomes that would directly and indirectly improve organizational effectiveness. Organizations may apply the relationships in this model to the workplace in order to help, facilitate, and maintain employee engagement. For example, if organizations provide their employees with clear expectations and performance feedback (organizational antecedents) and help them maintain or improve self-efficacy and work-life balance (individual antecedents), employees will be engaged in what they do, have better in-role and extra-role performances, and experience lower turnover intention.

This conceptual model provides a basic framework for explaining how employee engagement is influenced and managed, and thus could have an impact on desired organizational outcomes. If your organization is interested in particular antecedents and consequences regarding employee engagement, you can use Worksheets 1-2 and 1-3 to create a customized model of employee engagement for your organization.

Worksheet 1-2: Employee Engagement Model in Your Organization

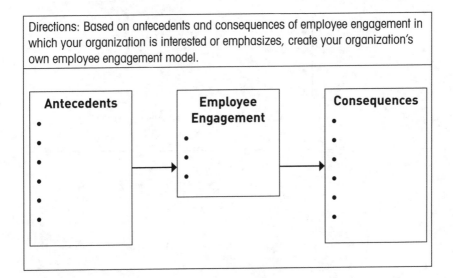

Worksheet 1-3: Antecedents and Consequences of Employee Engagement in Your Organization

Directions: Based on the suggested conceptual framework of employee engagement in Figure 1-1, think about what your organization is interested in or emphasizes regarding antecedents and consequences of employee engagement and list them here. In addition, write down any organizational policies, strategies, and/or activities pertinent to employee engagement that have been implemented by your organization.

Antecedents of Employee Engagement	Consequences of Employee Engagement	Organizational Policies, Strategies, or Activities Related to Employee Engagement
•	•	•
•	•	•
•	•	•
•	•	•
•	•	•
•	•	•

2
The Importance of Engaged Employees

William J. Rothwell

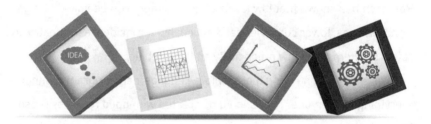

Employee engagement has galvanized attention in recent years. In good economic times, this becomes a focal point for retention strategies because engaged workers tend to be more committed to their organizations, work, and customers, and are thus less likely to resign. In bad economic times, engagement becomes a focal point for productivity enhancement, as workers feel demoralized by—among other things—pay freezes, layoffs, furloughs, and budget cutbacks affecting everything from supplies to technology. During these tough times, workers often feel trapped in bad situations—unable to be happy (or engaged) where they are, and unable to move to greener pastures elsewhere, thanks to limited work opportunities. Whether times are good or bad, employee engagement can—and should—be a front-burner topic that is linked to an organization's competitive advantage and an individual's productivity and morale.

Why Should You Care?

Employers and individuals should care about employee engagement, but, admittedly, they may have different reasons for doing so.

For managers, engagement is a way to combat its opposite—feelings of alienation, disempowerment, and low morale. When work is not meaningful, it can lead to apathy, and apathy can lead to disengagement at work. Research has shown that low levels of engagement can be linked to higher turnover rates, lower customer satisfaction, higher incidences of health and safety problems, and low productivity and profitability.

It is worth emphasizing that employee engagement programs cannot be everything to everyone. They should be created with good business reasons in mind, but the reasons, and thus the emphasis, of such programs may vary. Before starting an employee engagement program, employers need to be clear about what goals they want to achieve. Employers need to recognize that some goals need to take precedence over others, depending on the organization's current needs. By being selective, the employers will be better able to focus their efforts to create a cost-effective program that provides the highest value activities possible to achieve the goals and measure the results.

The following is a list of seven key reasons engaged employees are vital for an organization.

- Engaged workers are more likely to remain in their organizations and are less likely to resign.

- Organizations with engaged workers are more likely to enjoy financial success than those that do not.

- It is less likely that organizations with engaged workers will have to devote time and money to working out employee performance, turnover, and poor morale problems.

- Organizations with engaged workers are less likely to have trouble attracting the best people.

- Organizations with engaged workers have fewer work-related accidents.

- Organizations with engaged workers have lower stress-related problems. This is beneficial as stress is correlated with many problems that can lead to skyrocketing benefits and workers' compensation costs, including drug abuse, alcoholism, domestic violence, cancer, heart disease, and other health-related problems.

- Organizations with engaged workers are more likely to have loyal, committed customers; whereas organizations with a high percentage of disengaged workers are more likely to have problems with retaining customer loyalty.

On the other hand, workers care about employee engagement for many different reasons. The following are nine key reasons that individuals would want to work in an engaged organization:

- managers communicate what they want and why

- managers set positive examples

- workers see the value of what they do and who they serve

- workers see how their work impacts the customers

- the work is mentally stimulating

- there are future opportunities for career growth and advancement

- employees can be proud of what their organization does and what it stands for

- employees experience the value of useful collegial relationships with other people, who stimulate them to think and grow, in a psychologically comfortable (as opposed to threatening) environment

- employees enjoy supportive relationships with their supervisors.

Most employees say they want to be in a positive work environment where it is mentally stimulating, their efforts help others, and they are supported to grow and develop their potential. Consequently, an engagement program can be a way to strengthen the value of the work situation at an organization.

Employee Engagement in Various Settings

Employee engagement may be regarded somewhat differently depending on the setting. In businesses and academic institutions, for example, business leaders tend to focus on the practical aspects of engagement, simply wanting to achieve better results. Academics are usually interested in the key variables associated with engagement and wish to develop robust, validated ways to measure it.

Business leaders care about employee engagement for its value in focusing efforts on building an employment brand identity for their organizations and making the organization an employer of choice. They care about it because it may lead to greater productivity, lower turnover, and improved customer service. They can also use employee engagement as a focal point to integrate their talent management efforts to attract, develop, retain, and deploy the best people to achieve the best results at the lowest cost.

For academics, employee engagement can be a focus for study. Various efforts have been made to devise models composed of variables that can be tested for "fit" as part of a larger engagement model. For example, Vazirani (2007) developed a model that depicted engagement as encompassing such variables as: opportunities for personal development, effective management of talent, clarity of organizational values, respectful treatment of employees, organization's standards of ethical behavior, empowerment, image, equal opportunities and fair treatment, performance appraisal, pay and benefits, health and safety, job satisfaction, communication, family friendliness, and cooperation. These variables are related to feelings of value and involvement, and in turn are associated with employee engagement.

The Benefits of Focusing on Engagement

Focusing on engagement gives an organization a better ability to manage its human assets and to integrate its HR strategies. Engaged employees:

- are less likely to resign
- are more likely to speak positively of the organization to customers and possible job applicants
- are likely to attract talented people
- perform better
- are more highly motivated
- lead to higher organizational profitability
- lead to lower incidence of health and safety problems
- speak more positively about the organization to customers or prospective customers
- are more aligned with organizational values and ethics
- are more trusting of organizational management
- feel that they can play to their personal strengths more often.

3

Metrics and Instruments for Measuring Engagement

Rashed A. Alzahmi and Olga Buchko

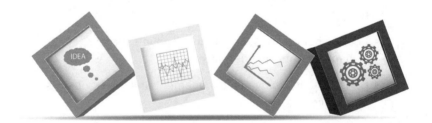

You Cannot Manage What You Cannot Measure

Measuring employee engagement is a business imperative. Many organizations measure their employees' level of engagement and strive to increase those levels because they believe high work engagement improves productivity, profitability, turnover, safety, and performance

(Little and Little, 2006). A number of researchers and organizations have argued that work engagement is a critical indicator of employee performance (Macey et al., 2009). Organizational leaders and managers want to measure results and establish accountability for actions and outcomes. According to Zoratti and Gallagher (2012), "The measured results become the focus of attention, the driver of investment and the means by which marketers track progress and performance" (p. 157). Therefore, it is essential for organizational leaders, employers, and decision and policy makers to understand how to evaluate and measure employee engagement levels in order to develop their employees and improve their organizations.

In short, measuring employee engagement helps organizational leaders, decision makers, and managers achieve the following:

- Discover which factors influence and drive employee engagement.
- Identify which employees or organizational units are the most engaged.
- Learn what the most engaged individuals, groups, or departments do differently.
- Consider a link between engagement and the company's key outcomes.
- Determine which factors block engagement or cause disengagement.
- Identify the company's best engagement practices.
- Adopt best practices and make them a model for the rest of the organization.

Furthermore, with the help of a number of established employee engagement instruments and metrics, organizations are able to collect information on how employees feel about their roles within the organization, the organization's leadership, and the organization itself (Harter, Schmidt, Killham, and Asplund, 2004; Schaufeli and Bakker, 2003).

Measuring Employee Engagement Domains

Work engagement is defined as "a positive, fulfilling, work-related state of mind that is characterized by vigor, dedication, and absorption" (Schaufeli et al. 2002, p. 74). The three constituting aspects of work engagement—vigor, dedication, and absorption—are at the core of a number of instruments created to help organizations ascertain whether or not their employees feel vigorous, energetic, happy, significant, and meaningful; possess a sense of satisfaction and an energetic connection with their work; or have any problems carrying out their responsibilities and dealing with their work requirements and organization's expectations (Schaufeli and Salanova 2007, p. 141). In the following two sections we will outline these instruments and provide some advantages and disadvantages to each.

The Shirom-Melamed Vigor Measure (SMVM)

The SMVM is one of the most reliable instruments for measuring work engagement, as it demonstrates the "connection of the individual to the work that she or he performs" (Gill, 2007, p. 4). According to Shirom (2004), vigor facets "are individually possessed" and "probably represent the three most silent domains of energy that humans possess—physical, emotional, and cognitive—relative to other types of energetic resources" (p. 74). This 12-item questionnaire, created by Shirom in 2005, covers the three facets of energetic resources that constitute vigor: physical strength, emotional energy, and cognitive liveliness. SMVM's 12 questions are set in a statement format and utilize a seven-point scale—ranging from "never or almost never" to "always or almost always"—to measure the frequency with which participants felt a certain way in the past 30 workdays.

This method has several advantages:

- reliability and validity in predicting important criteria—the instrument predicts turnover by providing information on employee engagement, job commitment, and satisfaction

- translations available: English, German, Russian, French, Polish, Spanish, Czech, and Hebrew

- simplicity: relatively simple to analyze and interpret

- wide usage: applicable to any organization and occupational area.

The SMVM method also has some disadvantages:

- lack of precision: some of the components may vary with time within the same individual

- limited translations: not available in every language.

For more information about this instrument visit Arie Shirom's website, www.shirom.org/arie/index.html.

The Utrecht Work Engagement Scale (UWES)

The UWES is another popular tool for measuring work engagement. Schaufeli and Bakker formulated the scale in 2003 at Utrecht University in the Netherlands. The UWES was originally composed of 24 statements that relate to the three aspects of work engagement: vigor, dedication, and absorption. The scale was later abridged to 17 of the original items, the UWES-17, when research found seven items to be unsound. There is also a version for students, the Utrecht Student Engagement Scale (UWES-S), in which some statements have been rephrased (Schaufeli and Bakker, 2003).

For each question, the participants select an answer from a seven-point scale (from 0 "never" to 6 "always or every day") to describe how frequently they feel a certain way at work. Individuals with a high vigor score are full of energy, zest, and stamina while at work. Those who score high in dedication strongly self-identify with their work and feel proud, enthusiastic, inspired, and challenged by their job. Those with a high absorption score are happily engrossed and immersed in their work, to the point where they have difficulty detaching (that is, they forget about time and pay no attention to what is happening around them). Participants who score low in any of these categories have the opposite characteristics.

The UWES has proven to be one of the most reliable and validated instruments in measuring work engagement. The advantages of this method include:

- user-friendly: easy to use and understand
- time effective: takes about five to 10 minutes to complete the survey
- wide scope of usage: can be widely used in international studies because of multiple translations (more than 20 languages)
- multi-group compatibility: several versions adapted for use with different occupational groups
- person-oriented: evaluates feelings and opinions rather than making assumptions
- free: can be used at no cost for non-commercial, scientific research.

No disadvantages were found to be associated with the UWES.

For more information about this instrument, visit www.arnoldbakker.com/news.php?id=58.

Employee Engagement Interview (EEI)

The EEI is an assessment tool designed to measure employees' engagement levels through an interview process. It aims to identify key elements that can help enhance employee engagement in the workplace. The EEI consists of open-ended questions, combined with a 1–10 rating scale, covering 17 different areas related to employee engagement. The interview can be conducted by an internal agent (the HR department) or by an external agent (a consulting firm). During the interview, the interviewee shares his or her opinions and latest experiences with the organization (see Worksheet 3-1 at the end of the chapter).

This method has several advantages, including:

- user-friendly: the EEI is easy to use and understand
- multi-group compatibility: can be used with different occupational groups
- person-oriented: it evaluates personal experience, feelings, and opinions
- possibility of data clarification: interviewer(s) can ask for clarification if an item is poorly stated
- meaningful data: open-ended questions lead to more descriptive data.

The EEI also has some disadvantages, such as:

- time consuming: the interview can take an hour or more
- data analysis: descriptive data is more challenging to analyze and identify key elements.

Measuring Job Satisfaction

Harter et al. (2002) defined employee engagement as an "individual's involvement and satisfaction as well as enthusiasm for work" (p. 269). For that reason, job satisfaction is an emotional state with significant implications on employee engagement and organizational functioning. Generally speaking, employees develop positive or negative attitudes and behaviors toward their work environment and employers based on their level of satisfaction. Positive job satisfaction is linked to organizational commitment, job involvement, and overall well-being, whereas negative satisfaction is linked to turnover and stress (Little and Little, 2006). Therefore, job satisfaction "can be considered an indicator of emotional well-being or psychological health" (Spector, 1997, p. 2). According to Ellickson (2002), job satisfaction is correlated with positive productivity, organizational commitment and effectiveness, and lower absenteeism and turnover. Thus, assessing employees' job satisfaction can help organizations evaluate employees' work morale and identify critical areas that need improvement.

The Gallup Workplace Audit (GWA)

The Gallup Workplace Audit (GWA), also known as the Q12, is the most widely used method for measuring employee engagement and workplace characteristics. Gallup empirically confirmed the association between employee engagement and organizational outcomes—such as profit, customer satisfaction, retention, safety, and productivity (Luthans and Peterson, 2002). Therefore, the GWA was developed to study the elements that positively influence work and learning environments—that is, employee engagement relative to desirable organizational outcomes (Harter et al., 2002).

Since the 1980s, the GWA underwent a series of modifications and improvements, which included a reduction in the number of interview items (from between 100 to 200 statements to just 12). The 12 items measure the employees' perceptions of their work environment and quality of management in their organizations or organizational units (Harter et al., 2002). According to Buckingham and Coffman (1999), the survey measures four theoretical constructs: What do I get? What do I give? Do I belong? How can we grow?

An overall satisfaction item—scored on a satisfaction scale, rather than an agreement scale—precedes the survey's 12 questions. The questions use a five-point Likert scale (from 5 "strongly agree" to 1 "strongly disagree"); the sixth response, "don't know/does not apply," is unscored; Bakker and Leiter, 2010. Employees with a high score are considered emotionally engaged in their work and the organization (Little and Little, 2006; Bakker and Leiter, 2010).

Advantages of the Q12 include:

- dependable: high reliability and validity
- simple: short and easy to use
- well-known: known globally and used in many different countries

There are some disadvantages, which include:

- limited use: reproduction and usage restrictions
- lack of cultural sensitivity: assumption that that employee engagement is the same in every country
- limited versions: not permitted for academic purposes

For more information, visit http://strengths.gallup.com/private/resources/q12meta-analysis_flyer_gen_08%2008_bp.pdf.

The Job Satisfaction Survey (JSS)

The JSS was originally developed for use in human services organizations. The survey is now widely used in all types of organizations, including public, nonprofit, and private. The JSS was designed to measure employees' attitudes toward nine aspects of their jobs: the nature of work, communication, relations with colleagues, training opportunities, work flexibility, payment, promotions, fringe benefits, and contingent rewards. Items are written in both directions—positive and negative—positively directed items indicate job satisfaction, whereas negatively directed items indicate job dissatisfaction. Each item is scored on a six-point Likert scale (from "strongly disagree" to "strongly agree"), and negatively worded items should be reverse-scored. The JSS can yield 10 scores (Spector, 1997; Astrauskaite, Vaitkevicius, and Perminas, 2011). Low scores on the scale indicate a high job satisfaction level.

Advantages of this method include:

- dependable: reliable and valid
- user friendly: easy to use, understand, and modify
- cultural sensitivity: applicable to any organization and different cultures
- multiple versions: not limited to human service organizations
- various translations: including Farsi, French, Hindi, Malay, Polish, Portuguese, Romanian, Spanish, Turkish, Vietnamese, and Urdu.

Disadvantages of this method include:

- data: interpretation and analysis of the data is difficult as the scale only provides general information in order to be applicable to more organizations
- limited certified translations: translations are not official because they are limited to the individual translator's use.

For more information about the JSS, visit http://shell.cas.usf.edu/~pspector.

Minnesota Satisfaction Questionnaire (MSQ)

The purpose of this questionnaire is to measure specific aspects of the work environment, obtain an individual picture of an employee's satisfaction, and understand the work aspects the individual is satisfied or dissatisfied with. The MSQ can also be used to counsel employees.

The original, long form of the MSQ includes 100 items that measure 20 facets of job satisfaction. Items are scored using a five-point scale (from 1 "very satisfied" to 5 "very dissatisfied"). The short form of the MSQ consists of 20 items and requires only five minutes to fill out, compared to the 15–20 minutes required to complete the original. However, the long form MSQ is more practical because it gathers much more information in a relatively short period of time (Weiss, Weiss, England, and Lofquist, 1967; Worrell, 2004; Ngo, n.d.; University of Minnesota Department of Psychology, n.d.).

Some of the advantages of MSQ include:

- dependable: reliable and valid
- user friendly: easy to use and understand
- wide application: applicable to a range of organizations and professional groups (managers, supervisors, and employees)
- ability to predict level of engagement: helps identify situations blocking employees from being engaged in their jobs.

Some of the disadvantages of this method include:

- complexity: a number of facets used in the instrument require a lot of knowledge and information
- time consuming: the original version is 100 items long
- discrepancy between the objective of the survey and results: information provided by the MSQ is more about the aspects of the individuals' job rather than about their job satisfaction.

For more information, visit www.psych.umn.edu/psylabs/vpr/msqinf.htm.

Measuring Job Burnout

Fundamental economic and technological changes have introduced new challenges and ever growing demands on the workplace. In order to be competitive and successful, an organization must address such issues through a variety of initiatives at a whirlwind pace, thus placing an enormous amount of stress on its employees. Work-related stress makes employees feel emotionally and physically exhausted, leaving them with little to no energy to devote to their work. They often feel disengaged and detached from their jobs and unable to perform at the level they once could. All these symptoms reduce feelings of personal accomplishment and efficacy and can ultimately lead to burnout (Maslach and Leiter, 1997; Maslach, Schaufeli, and Leiter, 2001).

Burnout is the antithesis of engagement, viewed "as a form of job stress with links to such concepts as job satisfaction, organizational commitment, and turnover" (Maslach, Schaufeli, and Leiter, 2001, p. 401). Maslach et al. (2009) defined burnout "as an unpleasant experience of work life with negative implications for performance, health, and well-being, [which] stands in contrast to a neutral existence at work" (p. 102). This reaction to physical, emotional, and/or interpersonal stressors is defined in terms of exhaustion, cynicism, and inefficacy (Maslach et al., 2001). Burnout is recognized as a critical problem across many different countries and within a variety of occupations (Maslach, Leiter, and Schaufeli, 2009). Therefore, organizational leaders and HR professionals utilize a number of instruments to assess the impact of major organizational initiatives on employees and prevent the consequences of burnout. The following sections will outline some of these measures and list some of the advantages and disadvantages associated with each.

The Maslach Burnout Inventory (MBI)

The original MBI, known as the MBI-Human Services Survey (MBI-HSS), was developed in the late 1970s by Christina Maslach and her co-workers to measure burnout in healthcare and human services (Maslach and Jackson, 1981a, 1981b). Soon after the MBI was introduced, it became the gold standard and most widely used instrument for measuring burn-out. In fact, three other versions of the MBI have been developed since its initial publication—MBI General Survey (MBI-GS), MBI Educators Survey (MBI-ES), and MBI Student Survey (MBI-SS). The MBI-GS was developed for non-social service providers and occupations that are not largely people-oriented, whereas the MBI-ES and the MBI-SS were developed for educators and students, respectively (Maslach et al., 2009; Schaufeli et al., 2002).

The MBI survey consists of 22 items that address the three dimensions of burnout: emotional exhaustion, depersonalization, and personal accomplishment. Emotional exhaustion is characterized by feelings of being emotionally overextended and exhausted by one's work. Depersonalization is characterized by negative feelings and impersonal responses toward the recipients of one's services, care treatment, or instruction. Personal accomplishment is characterized by feelings of competence and successful achievement in one's work (Maslach et al., 2009). This survey is scored using a seven-point scale—respondents choose an answer (from 0 "never" to 6 "every day") based on the frequency with which they experience the feeling described in the survey question. High scores on a particular dimension indicate greater emotional exhaustion, depersonalization, and personal accomplishment, and hence a more substantial degree of burnout.

Advantages of the MBI methods include:

- dependable: reliable and valid
- popularity: most widely used survey for assessing burnout
- multiple translations: translated into Spanish, Malaysian, Russian, Japanese, and German, among others
- ease of administration: self-administered survey
- length: takes about 10 to 15 minutes to fill out.

The disadvantages include:

- uncertified translations: the translations are not official because they are limited only to the individual translator's use

- issues with score calculations: three dimensions of burnout can't be indicated by one score because they are not equivalent

- flexibility issue: the multiple versions of the survey can cause confusion

- data analysis and interpretation issues: calculating and interpreting results can be challenging.

For more information about the MBI, visit www.statisticssolutions. com/academic-solutions/resources/directory-of-survey-instruments/ maslach-burnout-inventory-mbi.

The Shirom-Melamed Burnout Measure (SMBM)

This instrument for assessing burnout was inspired by the work of Maslach and her co-workers and Pines and her co-workers. The SMBM is based on the Conversation for Resources Theory, which states that individuals have a basic motivation to achieve, retain, and protect the resources that they appreciate (Shirom and Melamed, 2005; Shirom and Melamed, 2006). These resources include physical objects as well as personal traits, life conditions, and energies. Stress occurs when there is a threat of loss or an actual loss of these resources. The SMBM was developed to assess the exhaustion or depletion of energetic resources of individuals at work.

The SMBM is composed of a 14-item questionnaire that focuses on three dimensions of burnout: physical fatigue, emotional exhaustion, and cognitive weariness. These dimensions are closely interrelated, and an individual can experience them separately or collectively. Participants are asked to report how often they experience these feelings at work; all items are scored on a seven-point scale (from 1 "almost never" to 7 "almost always"). The calculation of scores in the SMBM is similar to that of the UWES—the total score is averaged by dividing by the number of items in the domain. High average scores indicate burnout severity; expert help may be necessary for those individuals.

Some of the advantages of the SMBM include:

- dependable: the instrument has been tested in various studies and countries
- translations: English, German, Russian, French, Polish, Spanish, Czech, and Hebrew
- simplicity: easy to use and relatively simple to analyze and interpret
- wide usage: applicable to any organization and occupational group.

Some of the disadvantages include:

- lack of precision: relies heavily on the individual's feelings and mood, thus results may vary if taken on a different day
- limited translations: not available in every language
- late predictor tool: mainly for individuals who score high on the survey.

For more information about the SMBM, visit www.shirom.org/arie/index.html.

Scale of Work Engagement and Burnout (SWEBO)

The SWEBO, created by Hultell and Gustavsson in 2007, is a relatively new tool for measuring an employee's state of burnout and work engagement. The instrument is comprised of two parts—one for measuring the three dimensions of burnout (exhaustion, disengagement, and inattentiveness) and another for measuring the three dimensions of work engagement (vigor, dedication, and absorption). Each segment has a total of nine items, which are rated using a four-point frequency response format (from 1 "not at all" to 4 "all the time"). The main focus is to understand what participants experienced and how they felt during the preceding two weeks—a timeframe often used when measuring depression (Hultell and Gustavsson, 2010).

Some advantages of the SWEBO method are:

- dependable: reliable and valid

- convenience: consists of two independent instruments that can be used separately—one to measure burnout and one to measure work engagement.

The disadvantages include:

- limited translations: only available in Swedish and English

- lack of popularity: not well-known, so it's not widely used.

For more information about the instrument, visit http://search.ki.se/search.do?q=swebo&lang=en&mode=profile_en.

Worksheet 3-1: Employee Engagement Interview (EEI)

Employee Name:	Last Review Date:
Job Title:	Date Issued:
Department:	Date Due:
Manager:	Time (from–to):

The Employee Engagement Interview (EEI) uses an open-ended interview combined with a *1–10* rating scale to measure an employee's engagement level for the period she has been working in the organization. The assessment examines 17 different areas that influence an employee's engagement level. The interviewee is expected to respond with special examples of how she handled different situations in the workplace. This assessment will highlight key areas of concern and enhance the employee's engagement level to support the organization's success. These questions can also be part of a performance review or interview. They can help the interviewer(s) define whether the worker possesses the skills and competencies required for a particular position.

1. Career Development (CD)

If you are asked to measure your level of satisfaction with career development opportunities provided at our organization ranging from 1 to 10 what score would you choose?

☐ 1   ☐ 2   ☐ 3   ☐ 4   ☐ 5   ☐ 6   ☐ 7   ☐ 8   ☐ 9   ☐ 10

Possible follow up questions:	• Have you discussed your career development plan with your supervisor recently? • What decisions were made? • Could you, please, tell us how our organization can help you develop your career?
Answer:	Describe the circumstances of the situation, your actions during the situation, and the results of your actions.

2. Communication (CM)	
If you are asked to measure your level of satisfaction with communication in your unit ranging from 1 to 10 what score would you choose? ☐ 1 ☐ 2 ☐ 3 ☐ 4 ☐ 5 ☐ 6 ☐ 7 ☐ 8 ☐ 9 ☐ 10	
Possible follow up questions:	• While working here have you ever had difficulties with understanding what your supervisor/manager tries to communicate you? • If so, how it was resolved? • In your opinion what can contribute to encourage open and honest two-way communication between the manager/supervisor and you/each employee?
Answer:	Describe the circumstances of the situation, your actions during the situation, and the results of your actions.

3. Compensation and Benefits (CB)	
If you are asked to measure your level of satisfaction with our current company's compensation structure and benefits package ranging from 1 to 10 what score would you choose? ☐ 1 ☐ 2 ☐ 3 ☐ 4 ☐ 5 ☐ 6 ☐ 7 ☐ 8 ☐ 9 ☐ 10	
Possible follow up questions:	• Have you ever had a feeling that you have not been fairly compensated based on your performance? • If so, could you, please, provide us with some examples. • What suggestions do you have for improvement?
Answer:	Describe the circumstances of the situation, your actions during the situation, and the results of your actions.

4. Decision Making (DM)	
If you are asked to measure your level of involvement in decision making ranging from 1 to 10 what score would you choose? ☐ 1 ☐ 2 ☐ 3 ☐ 4 ☐ 5 ☐ 6 ☐ 7 ☐ 8 ☐ 9 ☐ 10	
Possible follow up questions:	• Have you contributed to decisions and actions that affect your job recently? • If so, what was the situation and who encouraged you? • If not, what factors discourage you to provide your input? • What suggestions do you have to involve employees more in job-related decision making?
Answer:	Describe the circumstances of the situation, your actions during the situation, and the results of your actions.

5. Diversity (DV)	
If you are asked to measure your level of adaptation to our diverse community ranging from 1 to 10 what score would you choose? ☐ 1 ☐ 2 ☐ 3 ☐ 4 ☐ 5 ☐ 6 ☐ 7 ☐ 8 ☐ 9 ☐ 10	
Possible follow up questions:	• Have you ever experienced any of the following barriers to diversity while working at our organization: stereotyping, prejudice, or discrimination? • If so, what was the situation and how did you handle it? • In your opinion what can our organization do to manage our diverse workplace more effectively?
Answer:	Describe the circumstances of the situation, your actions during the situation, and the results of your actions.

6. Human Resource Functions (HR)	
If you are asked to measure your level of satisfaction with the support provided by the HR department ranging from 1 to 10 what score would you choose? ☐ 1 ☐ 2 ☐ 3 ☐ 4 ☐ 5 ☐ 6 ☐ 7 ☐ 8 ☐ 9 ☐ 10	
Possible follow up questions:	• Have you ever had a situation when you needed the support of an HR professional in order to solve the problem? • What was the problem? • Who was involved? • Did you get the assistance you wanted? • Do you have any suggestions for making partnership with the HR department more effective?
Answer:	Describe the circumstances of the situation, your actions during the situation, and the results of your actions.

7. Job Security (JS)	
If you are asked to measure your level of security ranging from 1 to 10 what score would you choose? ☐ 1 ☐ 2 ☐ 3 ☐ 4 ☐ 5 ☐ 6 ☐ 7 ☐ 8 ☐ 9 ☐ 10	
Possible follow up questions:	• Have you ever felt that your job security was threatened? • When and why? • What suggestions do you have to improve job security?
Answer:	Describe the circumstances of the situation, your actions during the situation, and the results of your actions.

8. Leadership (LD)
If you are asked to measure how clear, for you, the present direction of the organization is ranging from 1 to 10 what score would you choose?

☐ 1 ☐ 2 ☐ 3 ☐ 4 ☐ 5 ☐ 6 ☐ 7 ☐ 8 ☐ 9 ☐ 10

Possible follow up questions:	• Have you ever had a feeling that what you are doing isn't aligned with the direction the business is taking? • If so, please, provide us with some examples? • In your opinion what our organization can do to provide a much clearer sense direction and priority?
Answer:	Describe the circumstances of the situation, your actions during the situation, and the results of your actions.

9. Management (MN)
If you are asked to measure your level of satisfaction with your relationship with your immediate supervisor ranging from 1 to 10 what score would you choose?

☐ 1 ☐ 2 ☐ 3 ☐ 4 ☐ 5 ☐ 6 ☐ 7 ☐ 8 ☐ 9 ☐ 10

Possible follow up questions:	• Have you had the situation when you needed the support of your supervisor/manager in order to do your work right? • How fast and effective was the response to your request? • Do you think the company's present management style needs improvement? • If so, what recommendations do you have?
Answer:	Describe the circumstances of the situation, your actions during the situation, and the results of your actions.

10. Motivation (MT)	
If you are asked to measure your level of motivation at work ranging from 1 to 10 what score would you choose? ☐ 1 ☐ 2 ☐ 3 ☐ 4 ☐ 5 ☐ 6 ☐ 7 ☐ 8 ☐ 9 ☐ 10	
Possible follow up questions:	• Have there been changes in the company that have affected your motivation? • If so, what they were? • How do you describe the work environment or culture in which you are most productive and happy? • What would be the three greatest things that your employer could do to improve your/employee motivation?
Answer:	Describe the circumstances of the situation, your actions during the situation, and the results of your actions.

11. Recognition and Reward (RR)	
If you are asked to measure your level of satisfaction with the recognition and reward strategies ranging from 1 to 10 what score would you choose? ☐ 1 ☐ 2 ☐ 3 ☐ 4 ☐ 5 ☐ 6 ☐ 7 ☐ 8 ☐ 9 ☐ 10	
Possible follow up questions:	• Can you tell us about a recent time when you have been recognized, praised, or rewarded for your job? • Did the recognition and praise raise your individual productivity level and increase your work engagement? • How do you think the effective performers should be rewarded?
Answer:	Describe the circumstances of the situation, your actions during the situation, and the results of your actions.

12. Relationships With Co-Workers (RL)

If you are asked to measure your level of satisfaction with ongoing working relationships with your colleagues ranging from 1 to 10 what score would you choose?

☐ 1   ☐ 2   ☐ 3   ☐ 4   ☐ 5   ☐ 6   ☐ 7   ☐ 8   ☐ 9   ☐ 10

Possible follow up questions:	• Have you ever had a necessity to form a working relationship or partnership with someone from your unit to achieve an organization goal? • If so, how did you build that relationship or partnership? • How do you describe the work environment or culture in which relationships with colleagues contribute to effective cooperation and collaboration?
Answer:	Describe the circumstances of the situation, your actions during the situation, and the results of your actions.

13. Resources (RS)

If you are asked to measure your level of satisfaction with the resources allocation ranging from 1 to 10 what score would you choose?

☐ 1   ☐ 2   ☐ 3   ☐ 4   ☐ 5   ☐ 6   ☐ 7   ☐ 8   ☐ 9   ☐ 10

Possible follow up questions:	• Have you ever had a situation when in order to accomplish your work you needed resources that you did not have? • If so, what was the situation? • How it was resolved? • In your opinion, what is an efficient allocation of resources that contributes to employee motivation and satisfaction?
Answer:	Describe the circumstances of the situation, your actions during the situation, and the results of your actions.

14. Responsibilities (RP)	
If you are asked to measure how reasonable and fairly balanced your responsibilities are ranging from 1 to 10 what score would you choose? ☐ 1 ☐ 2 ☐ 3 ☐ 4 ☐ 5 ☐ 6 ☐ 7 ☐ 8 ☐ 9 ☐ 10	
Possible follow up questions:	• Have you ever had a feeling that you had difficulties with understanding what the organization expects of you at work? • Have you ever had a feeling that your work goals are not realistic and attainable? • If so, what would you recommend us to do in order to improve the situation?
Answer:	Describe the circumstances of the situation, your actions during the situation, and the results of your actions.

15. Satisfaction (ST)	
If you are asked to measure your level of satisfaction with your work ranging from 1 to 10 what score would you choose? ☐ 1 ☐ 2 ☐ 3 ☐ 4 ☐ 5 ☐ 6 ☐ 7 ☐ 8 ☐ 9 ☐ 10	
Possible follow up questions:	• Have you ever thought about leaving the organization? • If so, what made you think this way? • What would make you stay longer in the organization?
Answer:	Describe the circumstances of the situation, your actions during the situation, and the results of your actions.

16. Safety (SF)

If you are asked to measure your level of safety at work ranging from 1 to 10 what score would you choose?

☐ 1 ☐ 2 ☐ 3 ☐ 4 ☐ 5 ☐ 6 ☐ 7 ☐ 8 ☐ 9 ☐ 10

Possible follow up questions:	• For the period you have been working in our organization have you ever felt the need for a safer workplace? • Do you think you are provided with all the tools and equipment necessary to successfully and safely complete your job? • What do you think about the overall attention to safety within the workplace?
Answer:	Describe the circumstances of the situation, your actions during the situation, and the results of your actions.

17. Work-Life Balance (WB)

If you are asked to measure your level of work-life balance ranging from 1 to 10 what score would you choose?

☐ 1 ☐ 2 ☐ 3 ☐ 4 ☐ 5 ☐ 6 ☐ 7 ☐ 8 ☐ 9 ☐ 10

Possible follow up questions:	• For the period you have been working in our organization have you ever felt like having lack of the balance between work and personal life/family? • If so, what was the situation? • Could you please tell us how our organization can help you in balance your work and family commitments more effectively?
Answer:	Describe the circumstances of the situation, your actions during the situation, and the results of your actions.

The Visual Display of Quantitative Information

Make a line graph to display the data from the rating scales. The vertical axis represents the scale ranging from 1 to 10. The horizontal axis represents the number and abbreviation of the questions. This line graph can also be used to illustrate changes that have taken place over time.

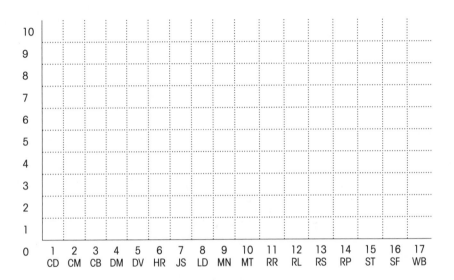

Feedback From the Interviewer:

Describe the level of the employee's engagement with the organization.

Provide recommendations on what should be done in order to increase the employee's engagement.

4

Strategies for Measuring Job Performance and Engagement

Naseem S. Sherwani

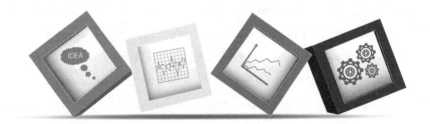

According to Groehler and Caruso (2013), an employee's feelings of enthusiasm for and involvement in her work are indications of engagement. This involvement occurs at work and in collaboration with colleagues—engaged employees feel recognized, encouraged, and supported. Engagement has emerged as a unique characteristic of high performers in an organization.

The global recession has caused slow economic growth in North American, Northern European, and Southern European countries. It has particularly influenced pay freezes, benefit cuts, and layoffs, which makes it difficult for the workforce to maintain a high level of engagement. At the same time, engaged employees are critical for business success, because they deliver better performance (AoN Hewitt, 2012).

Recent surveys from academic and corporate consulting/survey firms, such as Towers Watson, Kenexa, Hay, AoN Hewitt, and Gallup, have confirmed that employee engagement is an important determinant in improving performance and productivity and increasing profits in the private sector.

High Performance Versus Low Performance

Employee engagement increases when employees are given flexibility and the autonomy to implement changes within the company. In a TNS Employee In Sights survey of more than 145 organizations and 1.5 million employees, participants were asked questions about customers. In a comparison of high performing companies (HPCs; those who are leaders in their industries and demonstrate sustained financial growth) and other organizations, HPCs not only tended to have better relationships with their employees, but their employees were also focused more on customer satisfaction (TNS, 2011).

The analysis also found that a focus on the "ends"—or the end user, the customer—went hand-in-hand with a drive toward constant improvement and innovation. Employees in HPCs are much more dedicated to understanding the customer's current and future needs, and using that understanding to improve how they do their jobs and developing ways for the firm to make the necessary changes to be competitive. Employees in HPCs are also more market focused—their line of sight is not exclusively internal, but is focused externally on what is happening around them and their company. Finally, HPC employees are more energetic, look for new and better ways to do things, strive to improve performance, and feel the company as a whole has a vision for the future that is inspiring (TNS, 2011).

The payoff from an engaged workforce is highlighted in two studies conducted by Towers Watson (2011). In the first, engagement levels of 50 global companies were studied for one year. The results showed that companies with highly engaged employees saw a 19 percent increase in operating income and a 28 percent growth in earnings per share. Conversely, companies with low engagement experienced a 32 percent drop in operating income and an 11 percent decline in earnings per share. The second study looked at 40 global companies over a three-year period and found a 5 percent spread in operating margin and a 3 percent spread in net profit margin between companies with high employee engagement and those with low engagement.

Aligning Business Objectives With Employee Engagement

Supervisors and leaders need to align their business objectives with employee engagement endeavors, as well as define their goals, objectives, and strategies. This helps encourage employees to make superior contributions to the organization's goals. A well-communicated message builds trust that strategies will be implemented to achieve the employee's and the organization's goals (Hyman, 2012).

Normative benchmarking data of 120 countries and more than two million employees have established three key strategies of employee engagement that parallel the business objective (TNS Employee In Sights, 2011). These strategies reiterate that supervisors need to listen to employees' voices to develop new and better ways of operating their organizations. Employees demonstrate confidence in the ability of senior management to take action on their concerns. In addition, employees measure their leaders' inspirational capability, such as coaching, caring, and guiding, as an individual and as an employee to achieve the business objectives.

People-Focused Culture

The optimum utilization of resources enables the development of workplace environments in which people can vigorously work together. Similarly, a culture of support and mutual respect for co-workers and teams strengthens engagement, which leads to high performance in challenging times. A people-focused culture has always been important, but it is even more so now due to factors such as changing workplace demographics, work styles (Millennials work differently than Baby Boomers), technology (allows people to be faster and more efficient, but may serve to lower attention spans), and more concerted efforts to build trust among employees, supervisors, and management.

Engagement efforts can extend to training and development. For example, the voices of staff or employees as they deal with customers may be recorded for training purposes. A review of customer-employee conversations may generate ideas for further initiatives, adding value throughout public- and private-sector organizations. In other words, engaged employees have access to customers, leaders, and stakeholders within the organization through a variety of means. Their access to these learning opportunities empowers them to make important decisions and identify any gaps in the organizational culture. To overcome any such gaps, they interact with each other and share their interests, skills, and talents to make full contributions in the workplace.

Generally, organizations believe that high performers are the most engaged employees and will stay with the company longer, however a recent survey disputes that belief. According to Mark Murphy, CEO of Leadership IQ, a recent survey found that in "42 percent of organizations, low performers are actually more engaged than high and middle performers" (2013, p. 2). The findings from this survey show that the controversy regarding the low employee engagement of high performers needs further investigation.

Strategies to Improve Employee Engagement

Employees are a critical component to every organization, and their engagement serves as a barometer of organizational health (AoN Hewitt, 2012). By examining employee engagement, leaders, managers, and learning professionals formulate strategies that improve performance in the workplace.

Leaders

Leaders build an engaged workforce by using a bottom-up management approach that encourages employees to listen to their voices, respect their ideas, and make decisions and provide feedback at appropriate times.

Bennet Simonton (2012) who led more than 4,000 workers during 30 years in management positions put up a formal reference guide for engaging the workforce. An effective leader can use numerous techniques like group meetings and one-on-one interactions to increase productivity as much as 500 percent per person, raise the morale, build innovations, motivate poor performers into high performers, and create a culture of committed workforce.

Employee engagement is a two-way process in that leaders must believe in employees and employees must embrace top leadership buy-in. Leaders ensure strong support of adequate resources to achieve important goals. They also need to have open discussions about the factors that help high performers stay with the company.

Top leadership needs to take cautious steps, such as offering flex time, exposure to the latest technology, and training services, as well as giving clear direction about individual tasks and keeping team members fully informed. This will help to change and improve the behaviors of long-tenured employees in performing their jobs more effectively. Moreover, organizational leaders need to address engagement issues instantly rather than waiting for a one-year performance review (Campeau, 2012), as this is the most effective strategy to building an agile workforce.

Learning Professionals

The learning organization needs to make continuous efforts to provide learning and performance opportunities according to each employee's needs and the organization's culture.

An organization's investment in the overall well-being of an employee brings numerous benefits in terms of employee engagement—it improves the workers' physical health, makes them more likely to contribute to the community, helps them understand how to manage their finances, gets their career on the right track, and helps them to have better relationships with their loved ones (Rath, 2013).

Managers

Managers can significantly influence engagement levels through their communication and perspective. Unfortunately, the manager's role has not been reflected positively in the workplace. The negative attitude of managers breaks down the manager-employee relationships and increases stress among employees, especially about job insecurity and lack of trust. Claude Balthazard, director of HR excellence emphasized, "The key is not to point out the negative consequences of problem behaviours, but rather to convince the problem managers that results will be better if they change their ways" (HRPM 2011, p. 15). The Human Resource Professional Association (HRPA) survey indicated that a majority of Canadian professionals (73 percent) believe that managers who bully, speak inappropriately to staff, play favorites, or are disrespectful, are a significant problem in today's workplace—with negative implications on employee engagement, turnover, and workplace morale (HRPM, 2011).

Managers need to reflect back about their influence on employees' engagement levels by continuously communicating and asking for their perspectives. How managers interact, the expectations they set, and how they support their direct reports' work and development can change an employee from a low to a highly engaged colleague.

Both the employee and manager must agree to participate in the employee engagement process to ensure continuous development. Managers need to use a four-step performance correction model of describing the behavior, providing an example(s) of when the behavior was observed, describing the consequences of the undesired behavior, and developing a plan for resolving the issue (Dranitsaris and Hilliard 2013, p. 34).

The traditional performance appraisal systems actually hinder communications between managers and employees. The appraisal process is confrontational in several ways, especially given that it indicates supremacy on the managers' side and weakness by employees receiving the appraisal. The system allows managers to manipulate and score employees lower to reduce wage demands. While managers often cite performance appraisals and annual reviews as one of their most disliked tasks, performance appraisals continue to be a critical communication tool between the employee and the supervisor (Forster, 2011).

All in all, managers need to be trained to solve employees' engagement issues, while increasing their managerial performance as leaders in the organization. They need to develop action plans, with the employees' participation, in order to achieve short- and long-terms goals.

The Learning Organization

Learning organizations provide meaningful work, continuous attention on performance, and recognize the results of employees' work through a sustainable engagement process. After conducting a survey of 32,000 employees across 30 countries, the global professional services firm Towers Watson authored a report that indicated, among other findings, that employers should focus on "sustainable engagement." Such engagement was defined as the intensity of employees' connection to their organization based on three factors: the extent of their discretionary effort committed to achieving work goals, an environment that supports productivity in multiple ways, and a work experience that promotes employees' well-being.

Again the physical, emotional, and social well-being for the sustainable engagement of employees' is triggered by effectively enabling workers with internal support, resources, and tools; and creating a work environment that more fully energizes the employees (Birchall-Spencer, 2010).

CEOs who view themselves as "chief energy officers"—that is, encouraging, supportive, positive, and inspiring cheerleaders—can influence and engage employees with contagious energy, according to Tony Schwartz's November 2012 *Harvard Business Review* blog post, "New Research: How Employee Engagement Hits the Bottom Line." However, Claude Balthazard, Director, HRPA, warns that "some disengaged employees are disengaged because the work or work environment is not right for them, and some employees are disengaged because that is who they are" (2013).

Research shows that common characteristics of an engaged employee—regardless of the situation, her personality, or the engagement program—are whether or not the person is passionate, finds meaning in the work, contributes to the industry, has clear goals, and is doing her best to achieve these goals to make the organization successful. These qualities of a fully engaged employee make her feel good about herself (Cohen, 2013).

Companies should focus on hiring the right person for the job, buddying up the newly hired person with employees who have passion and pride in their work, and sharing stories of engaged employees to create a culture of engagement that leads to high performance.

The drivers of employee engagement and business results differ across different organizations and industries. For example, if a hospital focuses exclusively on improving the drivers of employee engagement, it should not expect to see an improvement in sales of its services. Instead it needs to focus on different sets of items that are currently driving the distribution of services. HR professionals should assess employee engagement as well as the drivers of business results in order to prepare their employees to achieve organizational goals and objectives.

Performance Appraisal

The purpose of performance evaluation is to improve employee performance to meet organization goals and strengthen management-employee relationships. HR professionals use hundreds of metrics to measure employee engagement and performance by tracking hours, retention, safety, training hours, and productivity, as well as conducting 360-degree performance evaluations.

Some HR practitioners disapprove of the traditional performance appraisal process. They consider it as counterproductive, divisive, and causing conflict among managers and employees. Controversial and subjective, the traditional performance appraisal tends to focus more on personality than on performance, with scoring systems treating subjective opinions as facts and paying attention to recent behaviors. Since performance evaluations are traditionally done annually, the employee's true performance over the year is obscured (Forster, 2011).

Managers need to pay attention to three evaluation errors when conducting performance appraisals:

- overrating a favored employee or an employee who had high ratings on a previous appraisal (Halo Effect)

- allowing outstanding work (or unsatisfactory work) immediately prior to the evaluation to offset an entire year of performance (Recency Effect)

- overlooking individual performance and rating all employees, or groups of employees, the same (Cookie Cutter Effect) (Timmerman, 2010).

Forster Emerson Consulting developed the performance improvement tool, Continuous Collaborative Conversations, which defines collaboration as shared responsibility and accountability for performance—among employees, their managers, and the organization. This approach includes a structured conversation—using inquiry, feedback, and active listening—between the employee and her manager about achieving performance goals. Both review applicable measurements, identify what needs to be done to improve performance, and develop an action plan. The manager acts as a supporter and facilitator to improve employee performance (Forster, 2011).

Although conducting performance appraisals is a time-consuming and challenging task, it is a critical opportunity to drive higher levels of employee engagement that are aligned with the organization's mission and business objectives. Managers can use performance appraisals to enhance employee engagement by providing feedback, planning career development, and identifying and removing obstacles to effective performance (Timmerman, 2010).

Organizations need to identify key attitudes that lead to success or failure, as this information will assist leaders in accurately identifying, rewarding, and correcting behavior according to actual employee performance. Most yearly reviews are skills-based, which allows skilled employees with poor attitudes (the very worst kind of low performers) to be rewarded, while high performers remain unrecognized (Murphy, 2003).

Engaging low wage employees has become a priority area for HR departments. Low wage employees are the largest group in Canada—comprising 35 to 40 percent of all jobs. Low wage service employees are generally less educated, earn less, and have fewer benefits. Retail, nonprofit health sector, and hospitality organizations have reaped the benefits by engaging low paid employees. The best HR practices improve the bottom-line with happier, more productive, and satisfied staff regardless of industry (Young, 2011).

Walgreens, for example, has adopted a people strategy that applies to more than 240,000 employees. The company began a listening tour in 2010, and the town hall format has since expanded to include virtual meetings where team members can air their concerns and ideas to promote a sense of community. The ideas generated during these sessions create workable solutions to company challenges, which managers then use to build action plans. Every leader is also required to have check-ins as part of the annual management process. By giving employees performance expectations, which in turn help them align to the business objectives, employee engagement was improved. Walgreens has improved its attrition rate by boosting employee engagement as measured by the annual employee survey (Whitney, 2013).

Organizations like academic institutions prepare an annual work plan for each staff member that includes specific tasks and targets that employees will undertake. The work plan also identifies career development goals, as a way of motivating employees, as well as any training needs, which the institute then pays for. These work plans are informally reviewed mid-year with the respective supervisors, and a formal, written response is required at year-end.

Making Disengaged Employees Engaged

Kenneth W. Thomas and Walter G. Tymon Jr. (2010) developed a work engagement profile (WEP), which measures the four intrinsic rewards—meaningfulness, choice, competence, and progress—that individuals receive directly from their work. Interpretive information for the scores of each intrinsic reward includes building blocks for improving and strengthening that reward. The profile is a 24-item, self-scorable assessment that takes 12 minutes to complete. It includes a 20-page booklet with interpretive information on scores that offers actionable steps to increase levels of engagement with work and various positive outcomes for both the individual and the organization.

Workforce engagement and retention strategies measure employee satisfaction, commitment to the organization, pride, and advocacy provides an accurate assessment of employees' commitment and contribution to the success of the organization.

Supervisors need to constantly ask for their employees' input, while also acknowledging that their input may not be implemented. They should also provide positive reinforcement for a job well done and clear non-punitive feedback if an employee makes a mistake or needs to improve. Managers need to engage their employees by talking to them, asking how things are going, and letting them know that their door is always open if they need to talk.

We surveyed managers and chief executive officers (CEOs) of firms located in Hamilton, Ontario, from June to August 2013 by asking two questions about employee engagement:

- What do you do to engage your employees and improve their performance?
- What technique(s)/strategies do you use to engage your disengaged employees?

Some of their strategies for improving performance included:

- Link pay increases to each employee's performance.
- Review branch- and association-wide engagement strategies.
- Provide free counseling or mentoring or coaching services when employees need assistance.
- Encourage open communication with the employees about issues they seem to be having or complementing them on their success.
- Conduct yearly performance appraisals using a simple questionnaire regarding the operation of the office—strengths, challenges, and what as an employee can do to help to offset the challenges.
- Hold a staff meeting and give employees a chance to share what is going on in the organization.
- Interview the disengaged employees to identify why they are disengaged, work with them to put together a plan to engage them more in the organization, and then evaluate in three months to see if they are engaged.

Organizations can use a variety of checklists, surveys, and instruments to engage their disengaged employees to get results.

Work Engagement Versus Workaholism and Burnout

Workaholism is defined as "the individual's steady and considerable allocation of time to work-related activities and thoughts, which do not derive from external necessities" (Harpaz and Snir, 2003, p. 291). Burnout—a psychological term that refers to long-term exhaustion and diminished interest in work—also has important implications in terms of work performance. The cost of burnout is higher for employees and employers in terms of mental health problems, absenteeism, and lateness. Christina Maslach and Susan Jackson identified the construct "burnout" in the 1970s and developed a measure that weighs the effects of emotional exhaustion and a reduced sense of personal accomplishment. The Maslach Burnout Inventory uses a three-dimensional description of exhaustion, cynicism, and inefficacy (Maslach, Jackson, and Leiter, 1996). Employee engagement—by contrast—is characterized as energy, involvement, and efficacy (Maslach and Leiter, 1997).

Workaholism may result from a combination of job involvement with an obsessive-compulsive personality, which consists of six distinct traits: obstinacy, orderliness, parsimony, perseverance, rigidity, and superego. Workaholics have two behavioral components—they tend to engage in non-required work activities and actively intrude on the work of others (Mudrack, 2004).

Douglas and Morris (2006) identified three subcategories of hard workers: the materialist, the low-leisure, and the perkaholic. Most individuals make decisions about working for long hours when they are motivated by the work itself, income, leisure, and prerequisites. Thus hard workers can work long hours for relatively high job satisfaction, but also stop working when they want to and engage in another activity without feeling the pain of withdrawal.

The same cannot be said of workaholics, who "work hard, rather than smart"—being strongly motivated by the work by itself, but still gaining relatively low job satisfaction. Depending on the breadth of their interests, workaholics are dedicated, integrated, diffused, or intense—inclined toward work addiction due to past experiences and personality traits. Many have difficulty distinguishing work from the rest of their lives, which causes difficulties in their personal lives and even health problems. Others find it hard to tolerate inactivity, viewing leisure time with feelings of guilt or dread (Klaft and Kliener, 1988). Type "A" individuals, in particular, are extremely competitive, overly concerned with controlling their circumstances and themselves, and incapable of resting (Klaf and Kliener, 1988).

However, some workaholics are remarkably satisfied with their work and their lives, depending on a variety of factors, including family acceptance of their work habits, autonomy and variety in the workplace, the match between job requirements and personal skills, and their general state of health.

Reducing Workaholism and Burnout

Workaholics often do not feel that they are workaholics, which makes it difficult to get them any treatment. However, workaholics must take the initiative to get better. They need to ask for help—making use of supportive workplace policies (such as flexible work arrangements), asking family members for help at home, and seeking assistance from a doctor if physical and mental health start to suffer (Galt, 2007). Balancing work and personal priorities is also important. A 2007 survey by Desjardins Financial Security showed that while 81 percent of Canadians want to achieve work-life balance, only 27 percent believe that it is attainable and only 17 percent believe that society supports workers having a good work-life balance. According to the poll, when Canadians are stressed 43 percent do physical activities, 16 percent talk to someone they trust, 13 percent read a book, and 11 percent engage in a relaxing activity, such as yoga (*Vancouver Sun*, 2007).

Alexandar Falco and co-authors (2013) discussed possible steps to prevent workaholism, such as workplace changes to achieve a better work-life balance and approaches to identifying and treating workaholics. In addition, employers need to give their employees the control to arrange work hours around family commitments and sanction holidays when it suits their family schedules. They also need to allow for a fixed number of paid family emergency days (Galt, 2007).

Workplace well-being relates to all aspects of life—such as the employee's health and safety, physical environment, work-life balance, and opportunities for professional growth and development. Organizations can provide programs—which may include counseling and psychological services, quality circles, or organizational surveys—to help their employees deal with the primary causes of stress and help prevent employee burnout (Jackson and Schuler, 1983). In addition, managers, counselors, and therapists can assist employees by conducting one-on-one meetings to determine and treat the root cause of the stress, which could eventually lead to burnout.

5
Creating the Engaged Culture

Catherine Baumgardner
and Jennifer Myers

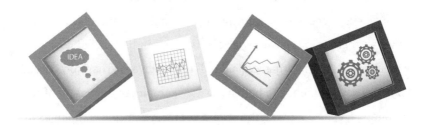

Chapter 4 explored the differences between workaholism and work engagement, the impact of work engagement, and the effect of burn-out on job performance was explored. Thus far the overall conclusion has been that engagement in work is a desired state. This chapter will focus on how to create an engaged culture so that the organization and employees can reap the benefits of that culture.

The journey to culture transformation is not one to be taken lightly. According to Maslach and Leiter (2008), the organization must decide and commit to an approach. That approach can either be organization-wide or individual. Maslach and Goldberg (1998) cautioned that many organizations choose the individual focus because it is often easier and less expensive to change people rather than an entire organization. However, it is suggested that the enduring model is a combination of approaches, which not only includes emphasis on the individual, but also encourages making fundamental changes to the overall organizational function so as to support the individual. This organizational approach requires very strong leadership and commitment to be effective. The world today is very volatile; those who can create organizations that thrive despite volatility are those creating a better work and employee life. Bakker (2009) explained that "many of today's organizations compete and try to survive on the basis of cutting prices and costs through redesigning business processes and downsizing the number of employees" (p. 3). However, there is a limit to what can be done in the way of cost-cutting without crippling the organization and its employees. Therefore, creating a positive environment and helping to boost employee engagement can be a challenge, especially with the severe challenges facing companies, their leaders, and their employees. With these challenges in mind, it's important to begin to understand the appearance of an engaged workforce.

An Engaged Workforce

As emphasized in chapters 1 and 3, engaged employees willingly give their time, energy, efforts, creativity, passion, drive, and knowledge to their organizations. Schaufeli et al. (2002) described the engaged workforce as one in which employees experience "a positive, fulfilling, work-related state-of-mind that is characterized by vigor, dedication and absorption" (p. 74). As defined by Bakker and Leiter (2008), vigor is characterized by high energy and mental elasticity. Dedication is being fully dedicated to and inspired by one's work. Absorption is being happily consumed by one's work. Therefore, an engaged workforce is one in which employees are happily achieving for the organization and for themselves.

In order to think about engagement in action, think about a business—for example, a restaurant. In restaurant A, the customer enters the establishment and waits to be helped. The customer waits for some time before finally approaching a staff member to see about getting seated. The customer is seated and waits at the table for 15 minutes before being greeted and offered a beverage. Once the order is finally placed, the customer waits another 30 minutes before the food is served and no one checks in with him while he is waiting. There are many people standing around without a lot to do and no one is smiling. They seem to be just getting through the day. When the food is finally served, it is cold and he has to send it back to the kitchen . . . and the saga continues.

In restaurant B, the customer is greeted immediately with a smile and, "How may I help you?" He is seated and within minutes, is offered a beverage. The food arrives quickly, is just the right temperature (hot foods hot, cold foods cold), and is delicious. The waiter is attentive and anticipates the customer's need by refilling drink glasses and offering any additional service. The place is abuzz with energy and everyone is smiling and focused on doing the best job they can.

The difference in these two situations is obvious. In restaurant A, no one seemed to be engaged at all in taking care of the customer, but in restaurant B, everyone was engaged in taking care of the customer. The individuals in restaurant A are not bad people—they just do not have the leadership or organizational support to give them the resources they need to be engaged for both the organization's benefit and their own.

While the environments in each restaurant are similar, restaurant B has what it takes to successfully engage its employees. The question is, what did the leadership do to consciously create the environment in restaurant B? To understand, it is important to reflect back on the JD-R model discussed in chapter 1.

This model suggests that leadership needs to very clearly understand the relationships between individual antecedents to work engagement, and organizational antecedents to work engagement, and make decisions that support the engaged employee state. For example, if the leader understands that the employee wants to be involved in meaningful work, is willing to direct her personal energies to the organization, and is dedicated to improving the organization (individual antecedents), then the leader can structure the employee's environment around placing her in the right job and giving her the control that she needs to do her job to meet organizational goals and antecedents. This congruence between individual and organizational antecedent is what creates engagement—both for the job and the organization.

However, just understanding this concept is not sufficient to ensure the creation and sustainment of an engaged culture. The leader's passion and focus must be evident throughout every leadership level in the organization, so that the everyone feels the same level of passion.

Organizations are reflections of the beliefs and attitudes of top leadership. This is supported by Sy, Cote, and Saavedra (2005), who found that members of a team experience a positive mood/outlook when leaders display a positive mood/outlook, as opposed to a negative one. In addition, teams lead by people with a positive mood showed a more cooperative effort while applying less effort, in contrast to teams with a negative leader who had the opposite experience. Leaders must recognize that their first-line supervisors are critical to the implementation

Figure 5-1: Conceptual Model of Employee Engagement

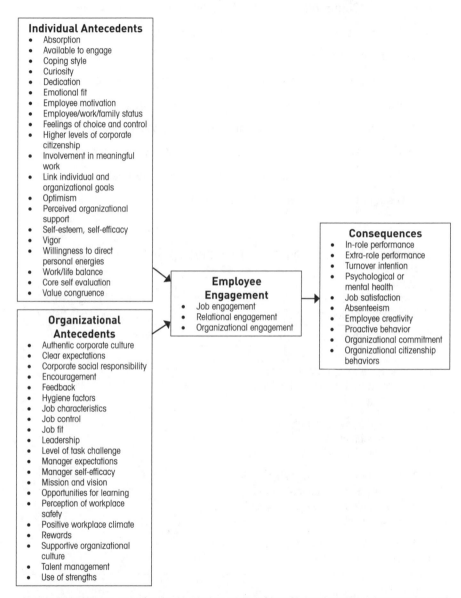

Individual Antecedents
- Absorption
- Available to engage
- Coping style
- Curiosity
- Dedication
- Emotional fit
- Employee motivation
- Employee/work/family status
- Feelings of choice and control
- Higher levels of corporate citizenship
- Involvement in meaningful work
- Link individual and organizational goals
- Optimism
- Perceived organizational support
- Self-esteem, self-efficacy
- Vigor
- Willingness to direct personal energies
- Work/life balance
- Core self evaluation
- Value congruence

Organizational Antecedents
- Authentic corporate culture
- Clear expectations
- Corporate social responsibility
- Encouragement
- Feedback
- Hygiene factors
- Job characteristics
- Job control
- Job fit
- Leadership
- Level of task challenge
- Manager expectations
- Manager self-efficacy
- Mission and vision
- Opportunities for learning
- Perception of workplace safety
- Positive workplace climate
- Rewards
- Supportive organizational culture
- Talent management
- Use of strengths

Employee Engagement
- Job engagement
- Relational engagement
- Organizational engagement

Consequences
- In-role performance
- Extra-role performance
- Turnover intention
- Psychological or mental health
- Job satisfaction
- Absenteeism
- Employee creativity
- Proactive behavior
- Organizational commitment
- Organizational citizenship behaviors

Note: Individual and organizational antecedents are adapted from "Antecedents to employee engagement: A structured review of the literature," by K. K. Wollard and B. Shuck. (2011). *Advances in Developing Human Resources, 13*(4): 433.

and follow-through of all engagement activities initiated by leadership. According to Cummings et al. (2012), leaders must also implement strategies designed to help others grow and cope with the ongoing flux of organizational change. There is often much excitement at the beginning of a change initiative, but if the changes in behavior are inconsistent across the organization, mid-level leaders will become disengaged with the effort, and their people will follow. Use the questions in Worksheet 5-1 to get an idea of the leadership style that is demonstrated in your organization. This will give you a much better idea of the barriers and enablers that exist, with respect to creating an engaging work environment.

Worksheet 5-1: Identifying Your Leadership Style

Directions: Based upon the description of leadership involvement in engagement offered here, think about your own leadership using the guiding questions below.	
Guiding Question	**Response**
1. Has my leader clearly described the focus of our organization? If so, what do I understand that focus to be?	
2. How has my leader given me the resources that I need to be engaged in our work?	
3. How consistent is the behavior of leaders in the organization with the overall leader? Do they support the same directions?	
4. How often does my leader ask me what I need to do my job?	

This confluence of the understanding of individual and organizational antecedents, combined with a clear and consistent vision, focus, and leadership behavior, is critical to the existence of an engaged work environment. The challenge is consistency, for while the concept is elegant, the implementation is often very tricky.

Building Engagement

The research findings of Maslach and Leiter (2008) highlight the complexity of building engaged environments. They were not able to find much published research on how well organizational interventions have worked, which they attributed to the following reasons:

- It is difficult to link individual data over time, as individuals may leave the organization between the implementation of change and the measurement of impact.

- It can be hard to distinguish the impact of internal change from the impact of external change.

- Interventions often require a change to the core of organizational work life, which is not something all organizations are willing to do.

- Companies may not allow research studies to be conducted because of the fear of confidentiality breaches.

However, there are ways that organizations can begin to better understand their current work climates as they can begin to tweak or build anew. As described in detail in chapter 3, there are a number of options for collecting the data needed to understand the current culture and help craft a direction toward the future—such as interviews, focus groups, observations, and survey instruments. In addition to those measures, other inventories can assist an organization in measuring engagement levels. The Areas of Worklife Scale (AWS) is one example. According to Maslach and Leiter (2008), this instrument identifies the six key domains of the workplace environment: workload, control, reward, community, fairness, and values. Coupled with management's assessment of supervision, communication, and skill development, and the administration of the MBI (Maslach Burnout Inventory), leadership using the AWS may receive a good overview of the organizational health. This, in turn, should give them the guidance needed to develop the appropriate management interventions.

The resounding conclusion is that leadership must be willing to ask the hard questions and to make the changes—within themselves and the organization—that are required to truly create an engaged workforce. A leadership directive for "everyone else to do it" will not result in a changed environment.

Researcher Arnold Bakker (2010) also weighed in on how to build and support the necessary culture for engagement, offering insights with respect to resources and leadership support. He advised that "job resources are assumed to play either an intrinsic motivational role because they foster employees' growth, learning, and development, or an engagement and 'job crafting' extrinsic motivational role because they are instrumental in achieving work goals" (p. 230–231). Leadership plays a vital role in the availability of job resources and the investment made in their professional development, as "job resources particularly have motivational potential in the face of high job demands" (Bakker, 2008, p. 16). Unfortunately, due to the volatility of the current economy, leaders are facing extreme limits on what they can provide to their employees. Xanthopoulou et al. (2009) defined job resources as "those physical, social, psychological, and/or organizational aspects of the job that (a) are functional in achieving work goals, (b) reduce job demands and the associated physiological and psychological costs, and (c) stimulate personal growth and development" (p. 236).

Job resources and the professional development of employees cost money, so it is critical for leaders to find a good balance. Van den Heuve et al. (2010) went further by addressing the negative impact of economic challenges on the climate in the work environment. These economic challenges often cause a reduction in resources, or a "do more with less" mentality, that can decrease employee motivation and their well-being. As Bakker found, "the main drivers of work engagement are job and personal resources. Job resources reduce the impact of job demands on strain, are functional in achieving work goals, and stimulate personal growth, learning, and development" (2008, p. 16). Additionally, through their work with the JD-R model, Bakker and Demerouti (2007) believe that job resources can motivate employees to improve performance, increase engagement, and decrease cynicism. With this knowledge, leaders can develop strategies and implement training that helps their employees foster engagement. By providing adequate job resources and giving employees what they need to be successful, leadership essentially giving them more reason to be motivated to accomplish their work in an engaged way.

Striking a Balance

Finding the balance between work and personal life is a critical element, because that is what keeps the employee from crossing the line to burnout. Whether burnout is the opposite pole of engagement or its own freestanding state is up for debate, however, it is agreed that burnout is detrimental to the employee and company.

Workaholics tend to over-do-it until their mind and body burn out. When burnout happens, they require time to rest in order to return to their pre-burnout state of being. It is a reflection of an extended, stressful work situation that has a significant negative impact on an individual due to prolonged stress (Demerouti, Le Blanc, Bakker, Schaufeli, and Hox, 2009). In an increasingly technological world, with 24/7 access to everyone, it is very easy for the lines between personal life and work life to blur. It is much too tempting to access work long after leaving the office, unless clear organizational expectations are in place. Remote employees or those who work primarily away from the job site are also prime candidates for losing their sense of balance and focus. "Accumulated research evidence shows that one's functioning at work may have a negative impact on one's functioning at home" (Demerouti, Bakker, and Voydanoff, 2010, p. 129). Demerouti et al. further explained that "researchers have long recognized that work and family are not separate, but rather interdependent domains or roles with 'permeable' boundaries" (p. 129).

So, with all this temptation, how does the leader ensure that the employee is not on a path to burnout? Maslach and Leiter (2008) suggested the following:

- Increase focus on individuals or groups that have a higher potential for burnout.

- Be alert to individuals who are experiencing high stress and are expressing concern.

- Match expectations of the workplace with reality.

- Work with the employee to create a balance between home-work demands.

As mentioned earlier in this chapter, the stress of an employee's work negatively affects them, their organization, their customers, and their families. Bakker, Demerouti, and Dollard (2008) indicated that "stress experienced in the workplace by an individual, may lead to stress being experienced by the individual's partner at home" (p. 901). This finding should come as no surprise, considering that both positive and negative emotions are often transferred to a person's spouse or partner due to their close living quarters and relationship. The conflict between work and family is also linked to the quality of family interactions, which holds true for both men and women. To date, the strategies implemented by employers have been designed to mitigate the impact of family on work behavior, with an eye toward improving employee productivity while on the job, but they have paid less attention to improving working conditions to mitigate the negative influence of work on family (p. 909). Therefore, it is critical for leaders to be aware of the views and attitudes of their employees, especially with respect to balance. Use Worksheet 5-2 to identify areas of imbalance for your own employees.

Worksheet 5-2: Identifying Engagement

Directions: Based on the description of the need for balance, think about your own organization by responding to the guiding questions below.	
Guiding Question	**Response**
1. Which groups of your employees might be at the greatest risk for burnout?	
2. List the key reasons why you believe they are at risk.	
3. Identify three things that you can do to prevent burnout from occurring in this group.	
4. Identify three ways that you gather information about factors that can trigger burnout in your employees.	

Being a leader is not just about telling people what to do. It is largely about understanding people's needs, motivations, and reactions to change. In doing so, the leader will be more effective in building and sustaining an engagement culture.

6
Overcoming Barriers to Build an Engagement Culture

William J. Rothwell

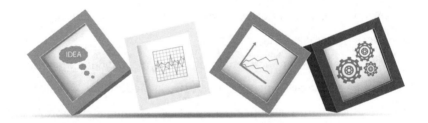

Improving employee engagement can be an endeavor fraught with many challenges.

What are some of those challenges? What can be done to overcome them? How can a culture of employee engagement be established and sustained? This chapter addresses these simple, but profound, questions.

What Are Some Barriers to Employee Engagement?

There are five possible barriers to employee engagement, including unclear understanding among workers or managers about what engagement is, management or employee cynicism about engagement, bureaucratic work rules, lack of work-life balance, and capricious management practices.

The first barrier is a lack of clarity about what engagement is. Some associate engagement with employee job satisfaction, morale, or even mere happiness. But it means much more than that. Engaged workers are satisfied with their jobs, motivated to do their best, satisfied with the work they do and the organization in which they do it, loyal to their organization, willing to say good things to others about their jobs and their organization, and proud of what they do and the organization in which they work (Quintana, 2011).

When management and employees are cynical about engagement it can also be a barrier. Cynicism is pervasive in modern life. A cynical view is generally negative, espousing a view that individuals are always selfishly motivated and act in line with self-interested motives. Those who question engagement on these grounds may regard it as a management fad that seeks to get people to work harder for less money, security, and praise—generally less of everything. In short, a true cynic will not see engagement as a genuine effort, but rather as the latest management trick to get workers to work harder for no reason.

Bureaucracy has the potential to be another barrier to engagement because in bureaucratic organizations, rules and procedures must be followed regardless of how appropriate they may be to a situation. Control, not results, is prized above all. In these settings, workers may lose hope and grow alienated because they have to work hard to have their ideas heard or get approval to make common sense changes.

A fourth barrier to engagement is lack of work-life balance. Some organizational leaders expect their workers to put their lives on hold, placing the organization first on all occasions. When economic conditions are poor, some managers—and other workers—feel obligated to work as many hours as possible to appear productive to their employers. Their greatest fear is that if they don't work extra hard, they may be the next victims of a downsizing. Under these conditions, it is impossible to be fully engaged because workers feel coerced, however subtly, to be on the job. But time on the job does not always correlate to productivity (or job security), because the value of time spent at work hinges on how it is spent (Vanderkam, 2011).

Capricious managers, who make decisions based on who asks rather than on facts, are the fifth barrier to engagement. They make decisions, but then change their minds quickly, and not always for obvious reasons. Workers faced with such managers feel disengaged because they do not feel heard—and do not believe their opinions are valued or supported.

What Can Be Done to Overcome the Barriers to Employee Engagement?

To overcome uncertainty among workers and managers about engagement, educate them. Give them whitepapers to describe what engagement is—and explain the solid business reasons for using it. You could also include discussions about engagement in meetings or in training programs and talk to managers and workers one-on-one about it.

To overcome management or employee cynicism about engagement, demonstrate why engagement is more than a management fad.

Describe the successes and benefits of placing a consistent emphasis on building and sustaining engagement and present it as an essential element in good management practice. But, make sure to point out that anything can be a fad if nobody remains committed to it.

To overcome bureaucracy, find a workaround solution. Do not let an adherence to unthinking rules wear you out. Fight a guerilla war if need be—undermine the bureaucracy by pointing out every occasion when the rules do not make sense. Refuse to let it get you (or others) down.

To overcome the lack of work-life balance, point out that people cannot work until they drop. Bring workers, and decision-makers, back to reality by pointing out that there is more to life than work.

To overcome capricious management practice, confront managers who change their minds and refuse to let them off the hook until they explain their rationale. In short, don't let them get away with it. Pointedly ask if decisions are swayed by who asked, rather than the merits of the situation or decision. Doing so once or twice will put otherwise capricious managers on notice that they will be confronted when they engage in biased decision-making.

Use Worksheet 6-1 as a tool in pinpointing possible barriers to employee engagement and brainstorm on ways to surmount those obstacles.

Worksheet 6-1: A Worksheet for Overcoming Barriers to Employee Engagement

Directions: Use this worksheet as a tool in planning ways to identify and overcome barriers to employee engagement. Review the barriers to employee engagement in the left column below and add any you feel are missing. Then, in the right column, discuss how to overcome the barriers. There are no "right" or "wrong" answers in any absolute sense, but some answers may be better than others.

Barriers to Employee Engagement		How Can the Barriers Be Overcome?
1	Unclear understanding among workers or managers about what engagement is	
2	Management and/or employee cynicism about engagement	
3	Bureaucratic work rules	
4	Lack of work-life balance	
5	Capricious management practices	
6	Other barriers to employee engagement in your organization (*list them*)	
7		
8		
9		

How Can a Culture of Employee Engagement Be Established and Sustained?

Many managers, when asked what they would like to do to improve their organizations, offer a simple answer: "change the culture." But what is corporate culture? How can it be changed? And more specifically, how can an organization's corporate culture be engineered to establish and sustain a workplace that fosters employee engagement? This section addresses these questions.

Defining Corporate Culture

When early anthropologists first visited locales where Caucasians had never (or rarely) been before, they needed a way to describe collections of group norms—unspoken rules of social interaction among members of a group—that were often quite different from their own. As people live and work together, they establish common understandings about what is good, bad, right, and wrong. But those understandings often vary across groups of people.

For instance, in what is now New Zealand, the Māori tribe believed it was desirable to hunt the heads of enemies. Some Australian tribes once engaged in cannibalism, based on the belief that eating one's enemies would allow the cannibal to absorb the powers of those they had eaten.

Culture describes the pattern of a people's beliefs about common issues in human life. Those issues include rites and rituals associated with (among others) birth, death, courtship, marriage, work, and spiritual life. Culture thus stems from a people's history and collective experiences. In a memorable and poetic definition, anthropologist Clifford Geertz defined culture in this way: "Believing, with Max Weber, that man is an animal suspended in webs of significance he himself has spun, I take culture to be those webs" (Geertz, 1973, p. 5).

Corporate culture is thus a term that refers to the unique pattern of beliefs that stem from the experiences of people in organizational settings. In Edgar Schein's (1992) classic definition, corporate culture refers to "a pattern of shared basic assumptions invented, discovered, or developed by a given group" (p. 9).

For Schein, and for the many others who have written about it, culture is extraordinarily difficult to change. One reason for this is that culture resides at a deep, nearly unconscious, level for those who live and work within it. There are also different levels of culture. The most superficial resides at the level of artifacts—such as physical artifacts (job descriptions and office furniture), or conceptual artifacts (mission statements, value statements, and sales slogans). A second level consists of rituals associated with joining the organization, leaving the organization, celebrating successes, and dealing with failures. The third and deepest level consists of group norms about "the way things are done around here," which are based on collective organizational experiences and thus represent institutional memory and collective wisdom.

Approaches to Changing Corporate Culture

A lot of research is focused around how to change corporate culture and, more specifically, how to change organizations. The statistics are not encouraging. According to various sources, 80 percent or more of organizational change efforts fail. The three most common reasons for failing are unclear goals for the change, unclear roles for those who are to be involved in the change, and unclear accountabilities for managers and workers (Mourier and Smith, 2001).

In the simplest sense, there are two major ways to change corporate culture—the top-down approach and the bottom-up approach.

The top-down approach is a programmed approach to change. In this method, organizational leaders establish a standard approach to making any change, regarding the organization much like a computer that can be programmed. (Some call this social engineering.)

There are many top-down models, but here is a basic example:

- Step 1: Scan the external environment to find the need for change.

- Step 2: Establish clear, measurable goals for the change.

- Step 3: Identify and enlist a group of people to champion and lead the change.

- Step 4: Identify those affected by the change (stakeholders) and take steps to address any sources of resistance.

- Step 5: Develop a step-by-step action plan to implement the change. This plan should include a consideration of how the change will be continuously communicated to all key stakeholder groups.

- Step 6: Implement the change.

- Step 7: Evaluate the change during and following implementation to make sure that the results match the goals.

This approach is driven from the top of the organization down, with leaders taking the initiative. One advantage of this approach is that it works well if all key decision-makers can be convinced of the need for the change. It is also fast. However, the approach may fail if leaders leave during the change effort and their successors do not own the gains made in the change. This method could also mean that there are fewer people to buy in to the change.

The bottom-up approach takes an organic approach to change. Organizational leaders guide the process, but allow workers to establish meaningful targets. Advocates of this approach, associated with organization development, regard an organization as an organic, growing thing.

Here is a basic example of a bottom-up approach:

- Step 1: Identify a reason for the change and find a consultant to help leaders guide the change process.

- Step 2: Assess the organization's problems, involving as many people as possible in that process.

- Step 3: Secure agreement on the problems and their relative importance to the organization.

- Step 4: Collect information from as many people as possible on solutions to the agreed-on problems.

- Step 5: Secure agreement on the solutions, ways to implement them, communication strategies, and measurable change objectives to be achieved.

- Step 6: Implement the change, keeping as many people as possible involved in the change process during implementation.

- Step 7: Facilitate the evaluation of the change during and following implementation to make sure that the results match the goals—and that goals are changed if conditions change.

This approach is driven from the bottom-up—leaders build an impetus for change, but empower workers to help frame the issues, set the targets, take the initiative, and be as involved as possible in implementing the change and measuring results. This approach works well if workers can be convinced of the need for the change. It is also more likely to secure long-term commitment. However, the approach may fail if leaders co-opt the process and workers feel that they have no voice in the change. It can also take somewhat longer to reach decisions, depending on how many people are involved in the decision-making process.

Building a Corporate Culture Where Employee Engagement Is Established and Sustained

Employee engagement can be implemented from a top-down or a bottom-up perspective. On the one hand, a top-down approach is likely to be managed like the implementation of a project. It can be fast, but may not be as well accepted as a bottom-up approach. On the other hand, a bottom-up approach is likely to be well-attuned to an engagement philosophy simply because workers and managers alike will be engaged in the formulation, implementation, and evaluation of the engagement program. It may require sustained commitment from senior leaders because involving people can be time-consuming, but the payoffs may justify the approach.

Use Worksheet 6-2 as a tool for planning the implementation of an employee engagement program using a top-down approach. Worksheet 6-3 is a useful tool for planning an employee engagement program using a bottom-up approach.

Worksheet 6-2: Plan Employee Engagement Using a Top-Down Approach

Directions: Use this worksheet to plan an employee engagement project based on a top-down approach. For each step below, describe exactly what to do in your organization to carry out the step. Add paper as necessary.

Steps in a Top-Down Approach	How could you implement the steps in your organization?
Step 1: Scan the external environment to find the need for change.	
Step 2: Establish clear, measurable goals for the change.	
Step 3: Identify and enlist a group of people to champion and lead the change.	
Step 4: Identify those affected by the change and take steps to address any sources of resistance to change.	
Step 5: Develop a step-by-step action plan to implement the change which includes consideration of how change will be continuously communicated to all key stakeholder groups.	
Step 6: Implement the change.	
Step 7: Evaluate the change during and following implementation to ensure that results match goals.	

Worksheet 6-3: Plan Employee Engagement Using a Bottom-Up Approach

Directions: Use this worksheet to plan an employee engagement project based on a bottom-up approach. For each step below, describe exactly what to do in your organization to carry out the step. Add paper as necessary.	
Steps in a Bottom–Up Approach	**How could you implement the steps in your organization?**
Step 1: Identify a reason for the change and find a consultant to help leaders guide the change process.	
Step 2: Assess the organization's problems, involving as many people as possible in that process.	
Step 3: Secure agreement on the problems and their relative importance to the organization.	
Step 4: Collect information from as many people as possible on solutions to the agreed-on problems.	
Step 5: Secure agreement on the solutions, ways to implement them, communication strategies, and measurable change objectives to be achieved.	
Step 6: Implement the change, keeping as many people as possible involved in the change process during implementation.	
Step 7: Facilitate evaluation of the change during and following implementation to ensure that results match goals—and change goals if conditions change.	

7
The Future of Employee Engagement

Catherine Baumgardner

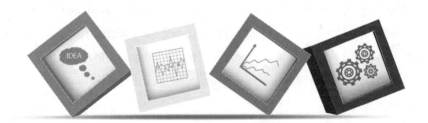

This book has laid out the research on and practical applications of employee engagement. Throughout, the case for engagement has been presented, and the challenges for keeping the employee's work habits and external life in balance have been emphasized. As noted in chapter 1, there are many different definitions for work engagement and the field is not in complete agreement about all aspects. What is agreed on is that the employee who has a high energy level and is enthusiastically involved in her work, has the potential to contribute more to the organization and her own personal well-being than do those who exhibit lesser traits.

Maslach and Leiter (2008) noted that work engagement thrives in settings that demonstrate strong connections between corporate values and individual values. With the idea that work engagement is a noble pursuit, this chapter highlights the academic and business models of engagement and the increasingly narrowing gap, expands upon the JD-R model, and outlines future considerations for engagement.

Bridging the Academic and Business Models of Engagement

Prior to the last decade, the majority of interest in employee engagement was seen in the consulting world. According to Schaufeli and Bakker (2010), engagement was utilized by consultants as a "catchy" label that covered very traditional concepts. They equated job characteristics (resources) to overall satisfaction, and essentially created a trendy aura around employee engagement. The business world then structured its arguments for employee engagement around traditional concepts that included:

- affective commitment (emotional attachment to the organization)
- continuance commitment (desire to stay with the organization)
- extra-role behavior (discretionary behavior that promotes the function of an organization).

Unfortunately, by doing so they captured neither scientific data nor the distinct value added by work engagement.

Eventually academia got more involved and began studying whether or not there was something unique about employee engagement. The research of Maslach and Leiter (1997, 2008) began with the premise that work engagement is a new concept, not a recycled one. They viewed engagement as the opposite of burnout, characterized by energy, involvement, and professional efficacy. Schaufeli and Bakker (2010) noted that work engagement "is defined as a positive, fulfilling work-related state characterized by vigor, dedication, and absorption" (p. 295). Academia went further by studying the differences between engagement and workaholism (which, if unchecked, can lead to burnout). Schaefeli et al. (2001) found that work is fun, not a compulsion, for engaged workers. Workaholics also give high on-the-job effort, but have a much different viewpoint. The engaged worker is happy, while the workaholic has a less positive view because he is compulsively compelled to perform with high effort.

Let's examine two employees—both work as grocery store managers. Employee A manages the produce department. He comes to work each day filled with energy and new ideas for how to keep his department and employees thriving and happy. His boss is very excited about the work that he is doing and readily accepts his new ideas, providing the resources he needs to deliver on his goals. He gets clear goals from his boss and he enjoys sharing those goals with his employees. Employee A is always happy to exert the extra effort to do his job, even if that means working longer hours sometimes. His boss recognizes him for his efforts and makes certain that he balances his work and home life by reminding him to head home if he's in the office too late. Employee A is also very happy at home, where he is actively involved in coaching his children's sports teams and golfing with his wife. Employee A is a very engaged and very happy worker.

Employee B manages the dairy department. She is obsessed with making her department better and works tirelessly to achieve her goals. She spends long hours in the store because she feels that long hours make her a better manager. She has been feeling very tired lately and does not look forward to coming to work. She feels that her job is draining her of her energy, but also feels that it's the price one pays for working hard. She usually gets home in the evening long after the children are in bed and rarely sees her husband before he is asleep. Her boss has tried to encourage her to better balance her life, but he is in the office all the time, too. He has also recently denied Employee B the opportunity to hire some help, citing budgetary concerns. Employee B is very engaged in her work, but finds it draining. She has crossed the line into workaholism and is on the verge of burnout.

These two workers both exhibit traits of the engaged employee. They are absorbed in their work and dedicated to the outcomes. Where they differ is on the vigor scale. Employee A is invigorated in his work in a very positive way, while Employee B is also invigorated, but in a negative way. In each case, the supervisor stressed the importance of balance between work and personal life. Employee A took it to heart, while Employee B ignored the advice. Thinking about the antecedents to work engagement, Employee A clearly has the necessary individual and organizational antecedents. Employee B is missing something— perhaps it is an emotional fit or it could be caused by the lack of example set by her manager.

The business model would argue that both employees are satisfied with their jobs because outwardly they are both very absorbed in their work. The academic model, however, teases out the unique state of work engagement by measuring the emotional quotient so that one can see the distinction between healthily absorbed and unhealthily absorbed. When considering how to more fully engage employees in the workplace, it is important to reflect upon their current situation. Use Worksheet 7-1 to give you some insights into your team and to build an action plan for change.

Worksheet 7-1: Work Engagement

Directions: Based upon the description of the engaged and burned-out employees, think about your own team and reflect upon the following questions:	
Guiding Question	**Response**
1. Which members of my team are highly engaged? What traits do I see that make me feel that way?	
2. Which members of my team are on the verge of burnout? What traits do I see that make me feel that way?	
3. Which members of my team are neither engaged or disengaged? Why do I feel that way?	
4. List some strategies for: • continuing to encourage engagement • encouraging more engagement • combatting burnout.	

Theory or Concept

With all the attention given to overall work engagement, it is logical to question whether or not it is a proven theory or if it is still in conceptual stages. Based upon the many different names and meanings for work engagement, as well as the different models in publication, it is safe to say that work engagement is still in the conceptual stages academically; however, very strong research is starting to move the model from concept to theory.

A current area of debate about work engagement is whether it is ongoing all the time, or can fluctuate—the engaged employee's commitment may fluctuate in short-term bursts—there may be days or moments where the employee is not as engaged. More research is being done regarding the day-to-day, moment-to-moment fluctuations in engagement in order to better understand this phenomenon.

However, research shows that job resources—social support, performance feedback, skill variety, autonomy, and learning opportunities—are positively correlated with work engagement (Bakker and Demerouti, 2008; Schaufeli and Salanova, 2007). The findings also indicate that a decrease in job demands has a positive correlation with the related psychological and physiological costs. Thus, fewer job demands result in more positive psychological and physiological outcomes for an employee. Research also has shown that employees with job resources are more functional in achieving their work goals and are stimulated toward personal growth, learning, and development. Hakanen and Roodt (2010) also found that job resources were the most important predictor of engagement.

Thinking back to Employee A and Employee B, it's evident that the first employee had the job resources to get the job done and hence, ended up engaged in his work.

Expanding the JD-R Model and Further Research

In chapter 1, an expanded look at the JD-R model was proposed. Unlike the JD-R model noted earlier in this chapter, the expanded view attempts to suggest a model of employee engagement on the basis of antecedents and consequences. Chapter 1 suggested that, by focusing on the factors that must be present for engagement, this model can help us focus more precisely on antecedent variables as predictors of positive engagement so that employers can enhance or change the current environment as indicated. As with the conceptual stages of the development of any theory, there are always other discreet types of analysis being conducted or other schools of thought being applied to the theory. This is certainly happening with employee engagement, most notably within the broaden and build theory, thriving theory, conservation of resources theory, and the gain spiral theories.

Demerouti and Cropanzano (2010) built on the theories of Frederickson (2001), which determined that positive emotions broaden people's ability to think outside traditional boundaries and wonder about possibilities, rather than seeing barriers to change. Frederickson (2003) also suggested that joy (positive emotion) encourages employee development, where employees are interested in learning new skills and forming relationships that will assist them in meeting their personal and professional needs. The question that remains, however, is whether or not the engaged employee really makes a difference to the organization. In their research, Halbesleben and Wheeler (2008) found that employee engagement predicts performance. Salanova, Agut, and Piero (2005) reported that organizational resources and work engagement could be used to predict the service climate for the organization, which was then a strong predictive indicator of performance and customer loyalty. The connection between engagement and outcome is critical to organizations that place value on engagement.

Another concept is the thriving theory (Spretizer, Lam, and Fritz, 2010). Research shows that people who thrive have a high level of vigor and bring new knowledge and skills to the workplace. Those who are thriving were also found to be more accepting of and adaptable to change.

The conservation of resources theory explored by Hobfall (2002) argues that individuals protect and accumulate resources over time, and that they learn skills and competencies to add value to the organization.

91

Coupled with the previously described theories, engaged employees see learning and development as key catalysts for helping them to grow and be valued by the organization.

When these theories are compiled in relation to employee engagement, the outcome is a gain spiral—when resources positively affect the work environment, employees become more engaged, but at the next level. Therefore, job resources lead to personal resources. According to Kohn and Schooler (1982), job and personal resources have a reciprocal relationship where individuals learn, and through learning have a more positive view of themselves. This more positive self-image then leads to the confidence to work outside the boundaries and be more innovative in the workplace. This cycle continues upward and keeps re-engaging the employee.

What does all of this research and its findings mean to the workplace? It gives the astute manager food-for-thought with respect to what he needs to know to best create an engaged workforce. With the strong correlation among job resources, engagement, and ultimate performance, one of the strongest messages to managers is to be aware of the job resources needed by employees. Management is not one-size-fits-all. Managers must be acutely aware of the needs of the individual, as well as the needs of the whole.

The Future Case for Work Engagement

So, where does work engagement go from here? With the strong correlations between engagement and outcomes, the quest for employee engagement is not going to go away. The authors of this book believe that the journey to prove the importance of engagement will continue and along the way, our understanding of the causal factors of engagement will be enhanced. According to Bakker and Leiter (2010), there is definitely a need to focus on a more universally accepted definition of work engagement. A major part of future research will be to come to some agreement on at least a core definition by both businesses and academicians. There is also discussion about absorption as a core measure of employee engagement, as there is some argument whether absorption is really an outcome of engagement. In other words, is an employee's absorption in their work a measure of their engagement, along with vigor and dedication? Or, is absorption in work the result of vigor and dedication to the work?

Another area of future research is the question around daily work engagement. For example, why do highly engaged employees sometimes have a moment or day when they are not engaged? Sonnentag (2003) suggested in her research that personality may affect the variability of work engagement, and proposed that making the work environment more consistent may be a strategy for evening out the engagement levels. Wreshiewski and Dutton (2001) and Wreshiewski and others (1997) looked at the concept of job crafting. This concept indicates that employees shape their own jobs as a way to find optimal balance between job demands and job resources. Each of these areas of future research poses the possibility that organizations and their leaders will have scientifically based methods for determining how to more precisely create the engaged workforce.

Therefore, there is little scientific evidence linking the impact of engagement on physiological health (Bakker and Leiter, 2010). However, awareness of the potential downsides of employee engagement is needed so that balance can be maintained. For example, Buehler, Griffin, and Ross (1994) found that those with high self-esteem (often a trait of the highly engaged) may underestimate the time for goal achievement, and may unwittingly increase the job demands and hence the stress upon themselves. Another caveat of the highly engaged worker is the tendency to allow their work-life balance to become uneven. The leader and the employee must work to preserve that balance, or run the risk of burnout. The other concern is whether or not a highly engaged work environment creates workaholics because high levels of absorption and dedication may predispose certain employees to tip the balance. This potential risk means that managers need to display a sense of work-life balance as well.

References

AoN Hewitt. (2012). 2012 Trends in Global Employee Engagement. www.aon. com/attachments/human-capital-consulting/2012_TrendsInGlobalEngagement_Final_v11.pdf.

Astrauskaite, M., Vaitkevicius, R., and Perminas, A. (2011). Job Satisfaction Survey: A Confirmatory Factor Analysis Based on Secondary School Teachers' Sample. *International Journal of Business and Management, 6*(5), 41–50.

Attridge, M. (2009). Employee Work Engagement: Best Practices for Employers. The Issue and Why It Is Important to Business. *Research Works, 1*(2), 1–12.

Bakker, A.B. (2009). Building Engagement in the Workplace. In R.J. Burke and C.L. Cooper (Eds.), *The Peak Performing Organization* (50–72). Oxon, UK: Routledge.

Bakker, A.B. (2010). Engagement and "Job Crafting": Engaged Employees Create Their Own Great Place to Work. In S.L. Albrecht (Ed.), *Handbook of Employee Engagement: Perspectives, Issues, Research and Practice* (229–244). Glos, UK: Edward Elgar.

Bakker, A.B., and Bal, P.M. (2010). Weekly Work Engagement and Performance: A Study Among Starting Teachers. *Journal of Occupational and Organizational Psychology, 83*(1), 189–206. doi:10.1348/096317909X402596.

Bakker, A.B., and Demerouti, E. (2007). The Job Demands-Resources Model: State of the Art. *Journal of Managerial Psychology, 22*, 309–328.

Bakker, A.B., and Demerouti, E. (2008). Towards a Model of Work Engagement. *Career Development International, 13*(3), 209–223. doi:10.1108/13620430810870476.

Bakker, A.B., and Demerouti, E. (2009). The Crossover of Work Engagement Between Working Couples: A Closer Look at the Role of Empathy. *Journal of Managerial Psychology, 24*, 220–236. doi:10.1108/02683940910939313.

Bakker, A.B., Demerouti, E., and Dollard, M. (2008). How Job Demands Influence Partners' Experience of Exhaustion: Integrating Work-Family Conflict and Crossover Theory. *Journal of Applied Psychology, 93* (4), 901–911. doi: 10.1037/0021-9010.93.4.901.

Bakker, A.B., and Leiter, M.P. (2010). *Work Engagement. A Handbook of Essential Theory and Research.* New York: Psychology Press.

Bakker, A.B., and Schaufeli, W.B. (2008). Positive Organizational Behavior: Engaged Employees in Flourishing Organizations. *Journal of Organizational Behavior, 29,* 147–154. doi:10.1002/job.515.

Bakker, A.B., and Xanthopoulou, D. (2009). The Crossover of Daily Work Engagement: Test of an Actor-Partner Interdependence Model. *Journal of Applied Psychology, 94*(6), 1562–1571. doi:10.1037/a0017525.

Bamford, M., Wong, C. A., and Laschinger, H. (2012). The Influence of Authentic Leadership and Areas of Worklife on Work Engagement of Registered Nurses. *Journal of Nursing Management, 21*(3) 529–540.

Baruch, Y., (2011). The Positive Wellbeing Aspects of Workaholism in Cross Cultural Perspective. *Career Development International, 16*(6), 572–591.

Beek, I.V., Hu, Q., Schaufeli, W.B., Taris, T.W., and Schreurs, B.H.J. (2012). For Fun, Love, or Money: What Drives Workaholic, Engaged, and Burned-Out Employees at Work? *Applied Psychology, 61*(1), 30–55.

Beek, I.V., Taris, T.W., Schaufeli, W.B., and Brenninkmeijer, V. (2014). Heavy Work Investment: Its Motivational Make-Up and Outcomes. *Journal of Psychology, 29*(1), 46-62.

Birchall-Spencer, M. (2010). Strengthens-Based Management Icon Tom Rath Reveals What Corporate America Doesn't Get About Employee Engagement. *The HR Professional,* (January/February), 37–40.

Blessing White. (2011). Employee Engagement Report 2011. Blessing White Intelligence, www.blessingwhite.com/content/reports/BlessingWhite_2011_EE_Report.pdf.

Blessing White. (2013). Employee Engagement Research Report 2013 Update. Blessing White Intelligence, www.blessingwhite.com/eee__report.asp .

Britt, T.W. (1999). Engaging the Self in the Field: Testing the Triangle Model of Responsibility. *Personality and Social Psychology Bulletin, 25,* 698–708. doi:10.1 177/0146167299025006005.

Buckingham, M., and Coffman, C. (1999). *First, Break All the Rules: What the World's Greatest Managers Do Differently.* New York: Simon and Schuster.

Buehler, R., Griffin, D., and Ross, M. (1994). Exploring the "Planning Fallacy": Why People Underestimate Their Task Completion Times. *Journal of Personality and Social Psychology, 67*, 366–381.

Campeau, M. (2012). The End of Reviews as We Know Them: Continuous Feedback and Career Coaching Can Help Managers to Get the Most From the Staff. *HR Professional* (July/August), 24–30.

CBI. (2012). *Facing the Future: CBI/Harvey Nash Employment Trends Survey 2012*. London: Confederation of British Industry.

Chughtai, A.A., and Buckley, F. (2011). Work Engagement: Antecedents, the Mediating Role of Learning Goal Orientation and Job Performance. *Career Development International, 16*(7), 684–705. doi:10.1108/13620431111187290.

Clinton, M., and Woollard, S. (2011). *Austerity or Prosperity? The State of HR In This Challenging Economic Environment*. London: Department of Management King's College.

Cohen, D. S., (2013). Talent Management—Are Employee Engagement Results Telling The Right Story? *The HR Professional*, (July/August), 40–41.

Cummings, G.G., Spiers, J.A., Sharlow, J., Germann, P., Yurtseven, O., and Bhatti, A. (2012). Worklife Improvement and Leadership Development Study: A Learning Experience in Leadership Development and "Planned" Organizational Change. *Healthcare Management Review* [ePub ahead of print]. May 2, 2012, www.ncbi.nih.gov/pubmed/22314974.

Demerouti, E., Bakker, A.B., and Voydanoff, P. (2010). Does Home Life Interfere With or Facilitate Performance? *European Journal of Work and Organizational Psychology, 19*, 128–149.

Demerouti, E., and Cropanzano, R. (2010). From Thought to Action: Employee Work Engagement and Job Performance. In A.B. Bakker and M.P. Leiter (Eds.), *Work Engagement: A Handbook of Essential Research* (147–163). New York: Psychology Press.

Demerouti, E., LeBlanc, P., Bakker, A.B., Schaufeli, W., and Hox, J. (2009). Present but Sick: A Three-Wave Study on Job Demands, Presenteeism, and Burnout. *Career Development International, 14*(1), 50–68.

Douglas, E.J., and Morris, R.J. (2006). Workaholic, or Just Hard Worker? *Career Development International, 11*(5), 394–417.

Dranitsaris, A., and Hilliard, H. (2013). Getting Beyond Employee Entitlement. Helping Employees Shift From Entitlement to Engagement. *The HR Professional*, (July/August), 32–33.

Dvir, T., Eden, D., Avolio, B.J., and Shamir, B. (2002). Impact of Transformational Leadership on Follower Development and Performance: A Field Experiment. *Academy of Management Journal, 45*, 735–744. doi:10.2307/3069307.

Ellickson, M.C. (2002). Determinants of Job Satisfaction of Municipal Employees. *Public Personnel Management, 31*(3), 343–358.

Falco, A., Girardi, D., and Kravina, L. (2013). The Mediating Role of Psychophysic Strain in the Relationship Between Workaholism, Job Performance, and Sickness Absence: A Longitudinal Study. *Journal of Occupational Environmental Medicine, 55*(11), 1255–1261.

Forster, W. (2011). Scrap the Performance Appraisal: It's Doing You More Harm Than Good. *HR Professional*, (May/June), 18.

Fredrickson, B.I. (2001). The Role of Positive Emotions in Positive Psychology: The Broaden-and-Build Theory of Positive Emotions. *American Psychologist, 56*, 218–226.

Fredrickson, B.I. (2003). Positive Emotions and Upward Spirals in Organizations. In K. Cameron, J. Dutton, and R. Quinn (Eds.), *Positive Organizational Scholarship* (163–175). San Francisco: Berrett-Koehler.

Gallup. (2013). *State of the Global Workplace: Employee Engagement Insights for Business Leaders Worldwide.* www.gallup.com/strategicconsulting/en-us/employeeengagement.aspx.

Galt, V. (2007). Workaholics Have to Learn to Just Say No. *The Globe and Mail,* (April 25), B18.

Geertz, C. (1973). *The Interpretation of Cultures.* New York: Basic Books.

Gill, D.S. (2007). Employee Selection and Work Engagement: Do Recruitment and Selection Practices Influence Work Engagement? PhD diss., Kansas State University.

Gorgievski, M.J., Bakker, A.B., and Schaufeli, W.B., (2010). Work Engagement and Workaholism: Comparing the Self-Employed and Salaried Employees. *The Journal of Positive Psychology, 5*(1), 83–96.

Groehler, L., and Caruso, K., (2013). *Using HR Metrics to Understand the Drivers of Employee Engagement,* 1–35. August 3, 2013, www.viapeople.com.

Hakanen, J.J., Bakker, A.B., and Schaufeli, W.B. (2006). Burnout and Work Engagement Among Teachers. *Journal of School Psychology, 43*, 495–513. doi:10.1016/j.jsp.2005.11.001.

Hakken, J.J., and Roodt, G. (2010). Using the Job Demands-Resources Model to Predict Engagement: Analysing a Conceptual Model. In A.B. Bakker and M.P. Leiter (Eds.), *Work Engagement: A Handbook of Essential Research* (85–101). New York: Psychology Press.

Halbesleben, J.R.B., and Wheeler, A.R. (2008). The Relative Roles of Engagement and Embeddedness in Predicting Job Performance and Intention to Leave. *Work and Stress, 22*, 242–256.

Harpaz, I., and Snir, R. (2003). Workaholism: Its Definition and Nature. *Human Relations, 56*(3), 291.

Harter, J.K., Schmidt, F.L., and Hayes, T.L. (2002). Business-Unit-Level Relationship Between Employee Satisfaction, Employee Engagement, and Business Outcomes: A Meta-Analysis. *Journal of Applied Psychology, 87*(2), 268–279. doi:10.1037//0021-9010.87.2.268.

Harter, J.K., Schmidt, F.L., and Keyes, C.L.M. (2003). Well-Being in the Workplace and Its Relationship to Business Outcomes: A Review of the Gallup Studies. In C. Keyes and J. Haidt (Eds.), *Flourishing: Positive Psychology and the Life Well Lived* (205–224). Washington, D.C.: American Psychological Association.

Harter, J.K., Schmidt, F.L., Killham, E.A., and Asplund, J.W. (2004). *Q12 Meta-Analysis*. Washington, D.C.: Gallup Consulting. http://strengths.gallup.com/private/Resources/Q12Meta-Analysis_Flyer_GEN_08%2008_BP.pdf.

Hobfoll, S.E. (2002). Social and Psychological Resources and Adaptation. *Review and General Psychology, 6*, 307–324.

Hultell, D., and Gustavsson, J. (2010). A Psychometric Evaluation of the Scale of Work Engagement and Burnout (SWEBO). *Work, 37*(3), 261–274. doi:10.3233/WOR-2010-1078.

Human Resource Professional Association (HRPA). (2011). "Problem" Managers Plague Canadian Workplace. *HR Professional*, (May/June), 15.

Hyman, G. (2012). Building Culture of Trust. *The HR Professional* (September), 39–41.

Jackson, S.E., and Schuler, R.S. (1983). Preventing Employee Burnout. *AMACOM*, 58-68.

Jackson, T., (2011). Human Capital: Focusing Engagement on Driving Performance. *HR Professional*, (May/June), 45.

James, J.B., Mckechnie, S., and Swanberg, J. (2011). Predicting Employee Engagement in an Age-Diverse Retail Workforce. *Journal of Organizational Behavior, 32*, 173–196. doi:10.1002/job.681.

Jeung, C.W. (2011). The Concept of Employee Engagement: A Comprehensive Review From a Positive Organizational Behavior Perspective. *Performance Improvement Quarterly, 24*, 49–69. doi:10.1002/piq.20110.

Jones, J.R., and Harter, J.K. (2005). Race Effects on the Employee Engagement-Turnover Intention Relationship. *Journal of Leadership and Organizational Studies, 11*(2), 78–88. doi:10.1177/107179190501100208.

Kahn, W.A. (1990). Psychological Conditions of Personal Engagement and Disengagement at Work. *Academy of Management Journal, 33*(4), 692–724. doi:10.2307/256287.

Karatepe, O.M. (2011). Procedural Justice, Work Engagement, and Job Outcomes: Evidence From Nigeria. *Journal of Hospitality Marketing and Management, 20*(8), 855–878. doi:10.1080/19368623.2011.577688.

Karatepe, O.M., and Ngeche, R.N. (2012). Does Job Embeddedness Mediate the Effect of Work Engagement on Job Outcomes? A Study of Hotel Employees in Cameroon. *Journal of Hospitality Marketing and Management, 21*(4), 440–461. doi:10.1080/19368623.2012.626730.

Ken, M. (2007). Canadians Working Harder, But Aren't Workaholics; Family and Health Rated Ahead of Work and Money: Final Edition. *The Vancouver Sun* (April 25).

Kim, W., Kolb, J.A., and Kim, T. (2012). The Relationship Between Work Engagement and Performance: A Review of Empirical Literature and a Proposed Research Agenda. *Human Resource Development Review.* Advance online publication. doi:10.1177/1534484312461635.

Kim, W., Park, C.H., Song, J.H., and Yoon, S.W. (2012). Building a Systematic Model of Employee Engagement: The Implications to Research in Human Resource Development. In J. Wang and J. Gedro (Eds.), *2012 Conference Proceedings of the Academy of Human Resource Development* (3916–3949). St. Paul, MN: The Academy of Human Resource Development.

Klaft, R.P., and Kliener, B.H. (1988). Understanding Workoholics. *Business, 38*(3), 37.

Kohn, M.L., and Schooler, C. (1982). Job Conditions and Personality: A Longitudinal Assessment of Their Reciprocal Effects. *American Journal of Sociology, 87*, 1257–1286.

Koyuncu, M., Burke, R.J., and Fiksenbaum, L. (2006). Work Engagement Among Women Managers and Professionals in a Turkish Bank: Potential Antecedents and Consequences. *Equal Opportunities International, 25*, 299–310. doi:10.1108/02610150610706276.

Laschinger, H.K.S., and Finegan, J. (2005). Empowering Nurses for Work Engagement and Health in Hospital Settings. *Journal of Nursing Administration, 35,* 439–449. doi:10.1097/00005110-200510000-00005.

Leading for Loyalty. (2005). Employee Engagement Assessment. www.leadingforloyalty.com.

Little, B., and Little, P. (2006). Employee Engagement: Conceptual Issues. *Journal of Organizational Culture, Communication and Conflict, 10*(1), 111–120.

Llorens, S., Bakker, A.B., Schaufeli, W.B., and Salanova, M. (2006). Testing the Robustness of the Job Demands-Resources Model. *International Journal of Stress Management, 13,* 378–391. doi:10.1037/1072-5245.13.3.378.

Luthans, F., and Peterson, S.J. (2002). Employee Engagement and Manager Self-Efficacy. *The Journal of Management Development, 21*(5), 376.

Macey, W.H., and Schneider, B. (2008). The Meaning of Employee Engagement. *Industrial and Organizational Psychology, 1,* 3–30. doi:10.1111/j.1754-9434.2007.0002.x.

Macey, W.H., Schneider, B., Barbera, K.M., and Young, S.A. (2009). *Employee Engagement: Tools for Analysis, Practice, and Competitive Advantage.* Malden, MA: Wiley-Blackwell.

MacLeod, D., and Clarke, N. (2009). *Engaging for Success: Enhancing Performance Through Employee Engagement.* London: Department for Business Innovation and Skills

Maslach, C., and Goldberg, J. (1998). Prevention of Burnout: New Perspectives. *Applied and Preventive Psychology, 7,* 63–74.

Maslach, C., and Jackson, S.E. (1981a). *The Modach Burnout Inventory.* Palo Alto, CA: Consulting Psychologists Press.

Maslach, C., and Jackson, S.E. (1981b). The Measurement of Experienced Burnout. *Journal of Occupational Behaviour, 2*(2), 99–113. doi:10.1002/job.4030020205.

Maslach, C., Jackson, S.E, and Leiter, M.P. (1996). *MBI: The Maslach Burnout Inventory: Manual.* Palo Alto: Consulting Psychologists Press.

Maslach, C., and Leiter, M.P. (1997). *The Truth About Burnout: How Organizations Cause Personal Stress and What to Do About It.* San Francisco: Jossey-Bass.

Maslach, C., and Leiter, M.P. (2008). Early Predictors of Job Burnout and Engagement. *Journal of Applied Psychology, 93,* 498–512.

Maslach, C., Leiter, M.P., and Schaufeli, W.B. (2009). Measuring Burnout. In C.L. Cooper and S. Cartwright (Eds.), *The Oxford Handbook of Organizational Well-Being* (86–108). Oxford, UK: Oxford University Press.

Maslach, C., Schaufeli, W.B., and Leiter, M.P. (2001). Job Burnout. *Annual Review of Psychology, 52*(1), 397–422. doi:10.1146/annurev.psych.52.1.397.

May, D.R., Gilson, R.L., and Harter, L.M. (2004). The Psychological Conditions of Meaningfulness, Safety, and Availability and the Engagement of the Human Spirit at Work. *Journal of Occupational and Organizational Psychology, 77*, 11–37. doi:10.1348/096317904322915892.

Medlin, B., and Green, K.W., Jr. (2009). Enhancing Performance Through Goal Setting, Engagement, and Optimism. *Industrial Management and Data Systems, 109*, 943–956. doi:10.1108/02635570910982292.

Mourier, P., and Smith, M. (2001). *Conquering Organizational Change: How to Succeed Where Most Companies Fail.* Atlanta: Center for Effective Performance.

Mudrack, P. (2004). Job Involvement, Obsessive-Compulsive Personality Traits, and Workaholic Behavioral Tendencies. *Journal of Organizational Change Management, 17*(5), 490–508.

Murphy, M. (2013). *Job Performance Not a Predictor of Employee Engagement.* Leadership IQ whitepaper, 1–11.

Ngo, D. (n.d.). Minnesota Satisfaction Questionnaires. The Human Resources. Hrvinet, www.humanresources.hrvinet.com/minnesota-satisfaction-questionnaire-msq.

Othman, N., and Nasurdin, A.M. (2012). Social Support and Work Engagement: A Study of Malaysian Nurses. *Journal of Nursing Management, 21*(8), 1083–1090.

Quintana, P. (2011). Barriers to Employee Engagement. Cause Related Learning. December 13, www.causerelatedlearning.co.uk/barriers-to-employee-engagement.

Rasch, R. (2010). *Engagement Trends Over Time.* Kenexa® Research Institute whitepaper, 1–3. www.kenexa.com/getattachment/1d2ded1d-4e1c-4820-a3c2-14b5185876ae/Engagement-Trends-Over-Time.aspx

Rath, T. (2013). Sustainability Employee Engagement. *Training and Development Magazine* (February 8).

Rich, B.L., Lepine, J.A., and Crawford, E.R. (2010). Job Engagement: Antecedents and Effects on Job Performance. *The Academy of Management Journal, 53*, 617–635. doi:10.5465/AMJ.2010.51468988.

Richardsen, A.M., Burke, R.J., and Martinussen, M. (2006). Work and Health Outcomes Among Police Officers: The Mediating Role of Police Cynicism and Engagement. *International Journal of Stress Management, 13*, 555–574. doi:10.1037/1072-5245.13.4.555.

Right Management. (2013). Employee Engagement. www.rightmanagement.ca/en/capabilities/employee-engagement/default.aspx.

Robinson, B.E. (1998). Spouses of Workaholics: Clinical Implications for Psychotherapy. *Psychotherapy: Theory, Research, Practice, Training, 35*(2), 260–268.

Rothbard, N.P. (2001). Enriching or Depleting? The Dynamics of Engagement in Work and Family Roles. *Administrative Science Quarterly, 46*, 655–684. doi:10.2307/3094827.

Saks, A.M. (2006). Antecedents and Consequences of Employee Engagement. *Journal of Managerial Psychology, 21*, 600–619. doi:10.1108/02683940610690169.

Salanova, M., Agut, S., and Peiro, J.M. (2005). Linking Organizational Resources and Work Engagement to Employee Performance and Customer Loyalty: The Mediation of Service Climate. *Journal of Applied Psychology, 90*, 1217–1227.

Salanova, M., Líbano, M.D., Llorens, S., and Schaufeli, W.B. (2014). Engaged, Workaholic, Burned-Out, or Just 9-to-5? Toward a Typology of Employee Well-Being. *Stress and Health, 30*(1), 71–81.

Salanova, M., and Schaufeli, W.B. (2008). A Cross-National Study of Work Engagement as a Mediator Between Job Resources and Proactive Behaviour. *The International Journal of Human Resource Management, 19*, 116–131. doi:10.1080/09585190701763982.

Schaufeli, W.B., and Bakker, A.B. (2003). *Utrecht Engagement Scale: Preliminary Manual.* Department of Psychology, Utrecht University, The Netherlands. Retrieved on September 23, 2013, www.beanmanaged.com/doc/pdf/arnold-bakker/articles/articles_arnold_bakker_87.pdf .

Schaufeli, W.B., and Bakker, A.B. (2004). Job Demands, Job Resources, and Their Relationship With Burnout and Engagement: A Multi-Sample Study. *Journal of Organizational Behavior, 25*, 293–315. doi:10.1002/job.248.

Schaufeli, W.B., and Bakker, A.B. (2010). Defining and Measuring Work Engagement: Bringing Clarity to the Concept. In A.B. Bakker, and M.P. Leiter (Eds.), *Work Engagement: A Handbook of Essential Theory and Research* (10–24). New York: Psychology Press.

Schaufeli, W.B., Bakker, A.B., and Salanova, M. (2006). The Measurement of Work Engagement With a Short Questionnaire: A Cross-National Study. *Educational and Psychological Measurement, 66*(4), 701–716.

Schaufeli, W.B., Bakker, A.B., and Van Rhenen, W. (2009). How Changes in Job Demands and Resources Predict Burnout, Work Engagement, and Sickness Absenteeism. *Journal of Organizational Behavior, 30*, 893–917. doi: 10.1002/job.595.

Schaufeli, W.B., Martinez, I.M., Pinto, A.M., Salanova, M., and Bakker, A.B. (2002). Burnout and Engagement in University Students: A Cross-National Study. *Journal of Cross Cultural Psychology, 33*(5), 464–481. doi: 10.1177/0022022102033005003.

Schaufeli, W.B., and Salanova, M. (2007). Work Engagement: An Emerging Psychological Concept and Its Implications for Organizations. In S.W. Gilliland, D.D. Steiner, and D.P. Skarlicki (Eds.), *Research in Social Issues in Management* (Vol. 5): *Managing Social and Ethical Issues in Organizations.* Greenwich, CT: Information Age Publishers.

Schaufeli, W.B., Salanova, M., Gonzalez-Roma, V., and Bakker, A.B. (2002). The Measurement of Engagement and Burnout: A Two Sample Confirmatory Factor Analytic Approach. *Journal of Happiness Studies, 3*(1), 71–92. doi:10.1023/A:1015630930326.

Schaufeli, W.B., Taris, T.W., LeBlanc, P., Peeters, M., Bakker, A.B., and de Jong, J. (2001). Maakt arbeid gezond? Op zoek naar de bevlogen werknemer [Does work make happy? In search of the engaged worker]. *De Psycholoog, 36*, 422–428.

Schaufeli, W.B., Taris, T.W., and Rhenen, W.V. (2007). Workaholism, Burnout, and Work Engagement: Three of a Kind or Three Different Kinds of Employee Well-Being? *Applied Psychology, 57*(2), 173–203.

Schein, E. (1992). *Organizational Culture and Leadership: A Dynamic View.* San Francisco: Jossey-Bass.

Shirom, A., and Melamed, S. (2005). Does Burnout Affect Physical Health? A Review of the Evidence. In A. Antoniou and C. Cooper (Eds.), *Research Companion to Organizational Health Psychology* (599–622). Northampton, MA: Edward Elgar Publishing.

Shirom, A., and Melamed, S. (2006). A Comparison of the Construct Validity of Two Burnout Measures Among Two Groups of Professionals. *International Journal of Stress Management, 13*, 176–200.

Shuck, B. (2011). Four Emerging Perspectives of Employee Engagement: An Integrative Literature Review. *Human Resource Development Review, 10*(3), 304–328. doi:10.1177/1534484311410840.

Shuck, B., and Wollard, K. (2010). Employee Engagement and HRD: A Seminal Review of the Foundations. *Human Resource Development Review, 9*(1), 89–110.

Simonton, B.S. (2012). *Leading People to be Highly Motivated and Committed.* Sun City Center, FL: Simonton Associates.

Society for Human Resource Management (SHRM) (2012). *2012 Employee Job Satisfaction and Engagement.* 1–88.

Sonnentag, S. (2003). Recovery, Work Engagement, and Proactive Behavior: A New Look at the Interface Between Nonwork and Work. *Journal of Applied Psychology, 88*, 518–528. doi:10.1037/0021-9010.88.3.518.

Sonnentag, S., Dormann, C., and Demerouti, E. (2010). Not All Days Are Created Equal: The Concept of State Work Engagement. In A.B. Bakker and M.P. Leiter (Eds.), *Work Engagement: A Handbook of Essential Theory and Research* (25–38). New York: Psychology Press.

Spector, P.E. (1997). *Job Satisfaction: Application, Assessment, Cause, and Consequences.* Thousand Oaks, CA: SAGE Publications.

Spreitzer, G.M., Lam, C.F., and Fritz, C. (2010). Engagement and Human Thriving: Complementary Perspectives on Energy and Connections to Work. In A.B. Bakker and M.P. Leiter (Eds.), *Work Engagement: A Handbook of Essential Theory and Research* (132–146). New York: Psychology Press.

Sy, T., Cote, S., and Saavedra, R. (2005). The Contagious Leader: Impact of Leader's Mood on the Mood of Group Members, Group Affective Tone, and Group Processes. *Journal of Applied Psychology, 90*(2), 295–305.

The American Society for Training & Development (ASTD) (2013). Sustainable Employee Engagement. *T+D*, (February), 20.

Thomas, K.W. (2009). Technical Brief for the Work Engagement Profile: Content, Reliability, and Validity. *Psychometrics*. http://www.psychometrics.com/docs/wep_tech_brief.pdf.

Thomas, K.W., and Tymon, W.G., Jr. (2010). Work Engagement Profile. *Psychometrics*.

Timmerman, P. (2010). Engaging Employees Through Effective Performance Appraisal. *Kenexa*, 1–3. Retrieved August 4, 2013, from www.kenexa.com/getattachment/c8b8c9dd-449c-4e24-b6c0-7eeba53230cc/Engaging-Employees-Through-Effective.

TNS. (2011). Employee Engagement to What End? High Performance Companies Keep the End in Sight. 1-6, http://tnsemployeeinsights.com/images/stories/tns/pdfs/TNS_2522-11BR_EmployeeEngage%5BPRINT%5D.pdf.

Towers Watson. (2011). *Global Workforce Study.* www.towerswatson.com.

Tracy, B. (2011). *Full Engagement: Inspire, Motivate, and Bring Out the Best in Your People*. New York: American Management Association.

University of Minnesota Department of Psychology (n.d.). Minnesota Satisfaction Questionnaire. www.psych.umn.edu/psylabs/vpr/msqinf.htm.

Van den Broeck, A., Schreurs, B., De Witte, H., Vansteenkiste, M., Germeys, F., and Schaufeli, W. (2011). Understanding Workaholics' Motivations: A Self-Determination Perspective. *Applied Psychology, 60*(4), 600–621.

Van den Heuvel, M., Demerouti, E., Bakker, A.B., and Schaufeli, W.B. (2010). Personal Resources and Work Engagement in the Face of Change. In J. Houdmont and S. Leka (Eds.), *Contemporary Occupational Health Psychology: Global Perspectives on Research and Practice* (124–150), Chichester: John Wiley.

Vancouver Sun. (2007). Canadians Working Harder, but Aren't Workaholics. *Vancouver Sun*, April 25, www.canada.com/story_print.html?id=a9aa3cc2-81b 8-4f88-9eed-0dadfd96eb9c&sponsor.

Vanderkam, L. (2011). How Many Hours Should You Be Working? *Fortune*, June 6, http://management.fortune.cnn.com/2011/06/06/how-many-hours-should-you-be-working.

Vazarani, N. (2007). *Employee Engagement*. SIES College of Management Studies Working Paper Series. Retrieved June 27, 2012, www.siescoms.edu/images/pdf/reserch/working_papers/employee_engagement.pdf.

Wagner, R., and Harter, J.K. (2006). *12: The Elements of Great Managing*. New York: Gallup Press.

Wefald, A.J., and Downey, R.G. (2009). Job Engagement in Organizations: Fad, Fashion, or Folderol? *Journal of Organizational Behavior, 30*, 141–145. doi:10.1002/job.560.

Wefald, A.J., Reichard, R.J., and Serrano, S.A. (2011). Fitting Engagement into a Nomological Network: The Relationship of Engagement to Leadership and Personality. *Journal of Leadership and Organizational Studies*. Advance online publication. doi:10.1177/1548051811404890

Weiss, D.J. , Weiss, R.V. , England, G.W., and Lofquist, L.H. (1967). *Manual for the Minnesota Satisfaction Questionnaire*. Minneapolis: Work Adjustment Project, Industrial Relations Center, University of Minnesota. www.psych.umn.edu/psylabs/vpr/pdf_files/Monograph%20XXII%20-%20Manual%20for%20the%20MN%20Satisfaction%20Questionnaire.pdf.

Whitney, K. (2013). At the Corner of People and the Business: A Profile. *Talent Management* (May), 44–47.

Wollard, K.K., and Shuck, M.B. (2011). Antecedents to Employee Engagement: A Structured Review of the Literature. *Advances in Developing Human Resources, 13*(4), 429–446. doi:10.1177/1523422311431220.

Worrell, T.G. (2004). School Psychologists' Job Satisfaction: Ten Years Later. PhD diss., Virginia Polytechnic Institute and State University.

Wrzesniewski, A., and Dutton, J.E. (2001). Crafting a Job: Revisioning Employees as Active Crafters of Their Work. Academy of Management Review, 26, 179–201.

Wrzesniewski, A., McCauley, C., Rozin, P., and Schwartz, B. (1997). Jobs, Careers, and Callings: People's Reactions to Their Work. *Journal of Research in Personality, 31*, 21–33.

Xanthopoulou, D., Bakker, A.B., Demerouti, E., and Schaufeli, W.B. (2009a). Work Engagement and Financial Returns: A Diary Study on the Role of Job and Personal Resources. *Journal of Occupational and Organizational Psychology, 82*, 183–200. doi:10.1348/096317908X285633.

Xanthopoulou, D., Bakker, A.B., Demerouti, E., and Schaufeli, W.B. (2009b). Reciprocal Relationships Between Job Resources, Personal Resources, and Work Engagement. *Journal of Vocational Behavior, 74*(3), 235–244.

Young, L. (2011). High Performance HR for Low Wage Workers: How to Manage a Service Sector Workforce? *HR Professional* (May/June), 22–25.

Zhang, X., and Bartol, K.M. (2010). Linking Empowering Leadership and Employee Creativity: The Influence of Psychological Empowerment, Intrinsic Motivation, and Creative Process Engagement. *The Academy of Management Journal, 53*, 107–128. doi:10.5465/AMJ.2010.48037118.

Zoratti, S., and Gallagher, L. (2012). *Precision Marketing: Maximizing Revenue Through Relevance*. Philadelphia: Kogan Page.

About the Authors

William J. Rothwell, PhD, SPHR, CPLP Fellow is a professor in the workforce education and development program, department of learning and performance systems, at the Pennsylvania State University. He has authored, co-authored, edited, or co-edited 300 books, book chapters, and articles. He is also president of his own consulting firm, Rothwell & Associates.

Before arriving at Penn State in 1993, he had 20 years of work experience as a training director and HR professional in government and in business. He has also worked as a consultant for more than 45 multinational corporations—including Motorola China, General Motors, Ford, and many others. In 2012, he earned ASTD's prestigious Distinguished Contribution to Workplace Learning and Performance Award. In 2013 ASTD presented him with the prestigious title of certified professional in learning and performance (CPLP) Fellow. He has visited China and many other Asian nations and has conducted in-house training, presented at conferences, conducted public seminars, taught MBA courses at famous universities, and served as an in-house change consultant.

His recent books include *ASTD Competency Study: The Training And Development Profession Revisited*, *Becoming An Effective Mentoring Leader: Proven Strategies for Building Excellence in Your Organization*, *Talent Management: A Step-by-Step Action-Oriented Approach Based on Best Practice*, the edited three-volume *Encyclopedia of Human Resource*

Management, *Lean But Agile: Rethink Workforce Planning and Gain a True Competitive Advantage,* and *Invaluable Knowledge: Securing Your Company's Technical Expertise-Recruiting and Retaining Top Talent, Transferring Technical Knowledge, Engaging High Performers.*

Catherine Z. Baumgardner, PhD, MHA, FACHE, is a faculty member in the health policy and administration department, College of Health and Human Development at the Pennsylvania State University, teaching the student cohort in the online master of health administration program. She is also president of Catherine Baumgardner & Associates, a full-service consulting practice focused on the organizational development of customer-focused cultures in the health professions. Catherine has nearly 25 years of experience at senior levels of healthcare management and consulting and has worked with hospitals and physician practices across the United States and Canada. She is a fellow in the American College of Healthcare Executives, and received a bachelor of science in business administration and a master's in health administration from the Ohio State University. She received her PhD in workforce education and development at the Pennsylvania State University, with an emphasis on organization development and human resources. Her research interests include demographic and workplace factors that influence work engagement among nurses and other health professionals. She is a popular speaker and author for industry related associations and professional associations.

Jennifer Myers is a fourth year PhD candidate in the workforce education and development program, with emphasis on human resource development and organization development at the Pennsylvania State University. She was also a graduate assistant and instructor at the professional personnel development center at Penn State. She earned a master's degree from Boston University and prior to arriving at Penn State was a special agent with the U.S. Air Force Office of Special Investigations. Her current research interests are work engagement, leadership development, and healthcare. She is the author and co-author of several publications in journals and books.

Woocheol Kim has a PhD in workforce education and development, with an emphasis on human resource development and organization development from the Pennsylvania State University. He has nearly six years of work experience in the fields of human resource development and employee relations as an assistant manager at Samsung Electronics, Korea. He earned a degree in mechanical engineering at Sung-Kyun Kwan University and a master's degree in human resource development strategy at Chung-Ang University in Korea. His research interests are positive change, work/employee engagement, performance improvement, and career development in organizations.

Olga V. Buchko is a PhD candidate in human resource development and organizational change, and comparative and international education, in the College of Education at the Pennsylvania State University. Prior to moving to the United States, she worked in education, project management and leadership roles in the Ukraine. In 2010 she came to the United States through the Hubert Humphrey Fellowship Program, a Fulbright exchange activity designed for experienced professionals from designated countries throughout the world. She earned a master's degree from Taurida National University in Simferopol, Ukraine, as well as South Ukrainian State Pedagogical University in Odessa, Ukraine.

Olga's broad research interests include cultural intelligence, global leadership, human resource development, and organizational change.

Naseem Saeed Sherwani has a PhD in workforce education and development, with a major in training and development from the Pennsylvania State University, and a master's degree in human resources development from Pittsburgh State University. She has designed training modules, delivered training instructions, facilitated working group sessions, and evaluated training activities at local and international levels. She has also worked on workforce development projects for the Institute of Research for Training and Development, Penn State Outreach and Extension, and the 7-State Change Agent States for Diversity in the Department of Agriculture and Extension project. She was also associated with updating the Workplace Learning and Performance Competency Model: Mapping the Future project with Rothwell & Associates. In addition, she has worked on community development projects in Canada, such as Affordable Housing and Homelessness and Ethno-Cultural Seniors through Volunteering Engagement. Her areas of interest include talent management, recruitment and retention, performance improvement measurements, occupational health and safety, employee engagement, and learning and performance at the workplace. She has a passion for ensuring that the workforce of tomorrow has the capacity and capability by assisting employers in tailoring effective professional development programs.

Rashed A. Alzahmi is a PhD candidate in workforce education and development, with an emphasis on human resources development and organization development at the Pennsylvania State University. He also earned a MS and BS in workforce education and development from Penn State, and an associate's degree in accounting from Pennsylvania College of Technology. Prior to his PhD study, Alzahmi worked in Abu Dhabi National Oil Company in the UAE for seven years where he was the head of the scholarship department. He was responsible for training and recruiting hundreds of talented individuals through various educational and training programs. He also served as a member in the board of trustees in the Glenelg School of Abu Dhabi for three years. His current research interests revolve around workforce planning, succession planning, human resource development, work engagement, organization development, and performance consultation.

Index

HOW TO PURCHASE ASTD PRESS PRODUCTS

All ASTD Press titles may be purchased through ASTD's online store at **www.store.astd.org**.

ASTD Press products are available worldwide through various outlets and booksellers. In the United States and Canada, individuals may also purchase titles (print or eBook) from:

Amazon– www.amazon.com (USA); www.amazon.com (CA)
Google Play– play.google.com/store
EBSCO– www.ebscohost.com/ebooks/home

Outside the United States, English-language ASTD Press titles may be purchased through distributors (divided geographically).

United Kingdom, Continental Europe, the Middle East, North Africa, Central Asia, and Latin America:
Eurospan Group
Phone: 44.1767.604.972
Fax: 44.1767.601.640
Email: eurospan@turpin-distribution.com
Web: www.eurospanbookstore.com
For a complete list of countries serviced via Eurospan please visit www.store.astd.org or email publications@astd.org.

South Africa:
Knowledge Resources
Phone: +27(11)880-8540
Fax: +27(11)880-8700/9829
Email: mail@knowres.co.za
Web: http://www.kr.co.za
For a complete list of countries serviced via Knowledge Resources please visit www.store.astd.org or email publications@astd.org.

Nigeria:
Paradise Bookshops
Phone: 08033075133
Email: paradisebookshops@gmail.com
Website: www.paradisebookshops.com

Asia:
Cengage Learning Asia Pte. Ltd.
Email: asia.info@cengage.com
Web: www.cengageasia.com
For a complete list of countries serviced via Cengage Learning please visit www.store.astd.org or email publications@astd.org.

India:
Cengage India Pvt. Ltd.
Phone: 011 43644 1111
Fax: 011 4364 1100
Email: asia.infoindia@cengage.com

For all other countries, customers may send their publication orders directly to ASTD. Please visit: **www.store.astd.org**.